Guit s
Handbook

by Amy Appleby and Peter Pickow

Cover photograph by Randall Wallace
special thanks to Jacqueline Torrance for editorial assistance

Order No. AM 967483
US International Standard Book Number: 0.8256.1828.2
UK International Standard Book Number: 0.7119.8504.9

Exclusive Distributors:
Music Sales Corporation
257 Park Avenue South, New York, NY 10010 USA
Music Sales Limited
8/9 Frith Street, London W1D 3JB England
Music Sales Pty. Limited
120 Rothschild Street, Rosebery, Sydney, NSW 2018, Australia

Printed in the United States of America by
Vicks Lithograph and Printing Corporation

Amsco Publications
New York/London/Paris/Sydney/Copenhagen/Madrid

Contents

BOOK 1: GUITAR OWNER'S MANUAL

The Guitar Family 8
  Acoustic Guitars 8
    Nylon-String 8
    Steel-String 8
    Twelve-String 8
    Pickups 10
  MIDI Guitars 11
  Specialty Guitars .11
  Electric Guitars .12
    Solid-Body 12
    Hollow-Body 12
    Semihollow-Body 12
Stringing 14
  Removing Old Strings 14
    Nylon Strings 14
    Steel Strings 14
  A Word on Stringing 15
  Replacing Nylon Strings 16
  Replacing Steel Strings 18
    Restringing a Tailpiece Guitar 18
    Restringing a Guitar with Bridge Pins 18
Tuning 20
  Relative Tuning 20
  Tuning by Harmonics 21
  Tuning to a Piano .22
Maintenance 23
  Cases 23
  Travel 24
  Storage 24
  Cleaning 24
  Lubrication 24
Repair 25
  The Frets 25
  The Tuning Machines 26
  The Neck 26
  The Finish 27
  The Body 27
Accessories 28
  Capos 28
  Humidifiers 28
  Peg Winders 28
  Tuning Aids 28
  Picks 29
  Straps 29
  Stands 29

BOOK 2: MUSIC THEORY FOR GUITARISTS

Reading Music 32
  Notes on the Staff 32
    The Treble Clef .32
    The Bass Clef 33
  Note Values and Rhythm 34
    Rests 36
    Notes and Rests 37
    Pickup Notes 37
    Dotted Notes and Rests 38
  Time Signatures 40
    $\frac{4}{4}$ Time 40
    $\frac{3}{4}$ Time 41
    $\frac{2}{4}$ Time 41
    $\frac{2}{2}$ Time 42
    $\frac{3}{2}$ and $\frac{4}{2}$ Time 42
    $\frac{2}{8}$, $\frac{3}{8}$, and $\frac{4}{8}$ Time 42
  Accidentals 43
    Sharps 43
    Flats 43
    Naturals 43
  Major Keys and Scales 44
    The Key of C Major 44
    The Sharp Keys 45
    The Flat Keys .48
  Compound Time Signatures 50
  More About Note Values and Rhythm 52
    Ties 52
    Extended Rests 53
    Pauses 53
    Triplets and Other Note Groupings 53
  Intervals 55
    Diatonic Intervals 55
    Chromatic Intervals 56
  Double Sharps and Flats 59
  Minor Keys and Scales 60
  Structure 64
    Repeat Sign 64
    Inverted Repeat Sign 65
    Da Capo 65
    Dal Segno 66
    Alternate Endings 66
    D.C. al Coda .67
    D.S. al Coda .67
    D.C. al Fine 68
    D.S. al Fine 68
  Accents and Articulations 69
    Staccato 69
    Accents 69
    Slur 70
    Phrase Mark 70
  Ornaments 71

Grace Notes 71
Trills 72
Tremolo 72
Turns 73
Mordents 73
Tempo 74
Expression 75
Dynamics 75
Reading Tablature 76
Hammerons, Pulloffs, Slides, and Bends 77
Other Tablature Symbols 78
Table of Notes 80
Chord Chart 82
Lead Sheet 84

BOOK 3: GUITAR SCALE DICTIONARY

Scale Basics 88
Major Scales 89
In-Position Major Scale Patterns 92
Modulating Major Scales 95
Modulating Major Scale Patterns 95
Minor Scales 98
Natural Minor Scale 98
Harmonic Minor Scale 99
Harmonic Minor Scale Patterns 99
Melodic Minor Scale 102
Melodic Minor Scale Patterns 102
Modes 105
The Dorian Mode 105
The Phrygian Mode 105
The Lydian Mode 105
The Mixolydian Mode 106
The Aeolian Mode 106
The Locrian Mode 106
Parallel Modes 107
Parallel Modal Scale Patterns 108
Transposing Modal Scales 110
Lydian Flat-Seven Scale 114
Lydian Flat-Seven Scale Patterns 115
The Chromatic Scale 116
Chromatic Scale Patterns 116
Pentatonic Scales 118
Major Pentatonic Scale 118
Major Pentatonic Scale Patterns 118
Minor Pentatonic Blues Scale 120
Minor Pentatonic Blues Scale Patterns 120
Major Six-Note Blues Scale 122
Major Six-Note Blues Scale Patterns 122
Blues Scale Variations 122
Major Six-Note Blues Scale 122
Major Six-Note Blues Scale Patterns 122
Minor Six-Note Blues Scale 124
Seven-Note Blues Scale 124
Seven-Note Blues Scale Patterns 125
Diminished Scale 126
Diminished Scale Patterns 126
Whole-Tone Scale 128
Whole-Tone Scale Patterns 128

Altered Scales 130
  Altered Scale Patterns 130
Pentatonic Scale Variations 134
  Tonal Pentatonic Scales 132
    Tonal Pentatonic Scale Patterns 130
  Semitonal Pentatonic Scales 135
Tap-On Scales 137
Open-String Scales 138
Scales with Harmonics 140
Ethnic Scales 141

BOOK 4: GUITAR CHORD DICTIONARY

Basic Chord Theory 146
  Chord Diagrams 146
  Major Chords 146
  Chord Inversions .147
  Minor Chords 147
  Minor Seventh Chords 148
  Augmented and Diminished Chords 148
  Major Sixth and Major Seventh Chords 148
  Table of Chord Symbols 149
Standard Tuning .150
  C Chords 150
  C♯/D♭ Chords 152
  D Chords 154
  D♯/E♭ Chords 156
  E Chords 158
  F Chords 160
  F♯/G♭ Chords 162
  G Chords 164
  G♯/A♭ Chords 166
  A Chords 168
  A♯/B♭ Chords 170
  B Chords 172
Open Tunings 175
  Open G Tuning (DGDGBD) 175
    Chords in Open G Tuning 176
  Open D Tuning (DADF♯AD) 187
    Chords in Open D Tuning 188
  D Modal Tuning (DADGAD) 198
    Chords in D Modal Tuning 199
  Dropped D Tuning (DADGBE) 200
    Chords in Dropped D Tuning 201
  D Minor "Crossnote" Tuning (DADFAD) 202
    Chords in D Minor Tuning 203
  Open A Tuning (EAC♯EAE) 204
    Chords in Open A Tuning 204
  Open C Tuning (CGCGCE) 206
    Chords in Open C Tuning 206

BOOK 5: GUITAR MANUSCRIPT PAPER

Chord Diagram Paper

Vocal/Guitar Tablature Paper

Guitar Tablature Paper

Guitar Owner's Manual

There are a dazzling variety of guitars in the world today—and dozens of different musical genres that feature acoustic and electric guitar. In the hands of different musicians, these instruments are able to produce a wide range of distinctive sounds and effects. In this book, you'll find an introduction to the important members of the guitar family. Here you will also find instructions on restringing and tuning your guitar, as well as some practical advice on routine instrument care and repair.

The Guitar Family

Whether you have an acoustic or an electric guitar, the principles of playing are fundamentally the same. So are most of the physical features of both instruments. This section provides an overview of the guitars commonly used today.

To learn about chords and tunings for the standard guitar, refer to *Book 4: Guitar Chord Dictionary.*

Acoustic Guitars

The guitar has a rich musical history spanning five centuries. Its widespread popularity is largely due to the fact that it is portable and easy to play. Today, the guitar is used by both classical and contemporary musicians—and is an integral part of the music of many cultures. With a range of over three octaves, the guitar is an expressive and versatile instrument, called by Beethoven a "miniature orchestra." Acoustic guitars come in a variety of shapes and sizes, but they all share the same basic characteristics shown in the diagram at right.

The first guitars had strings made from animal sinew (commonly called "cat gut"). Today, acoustic guitars can be divided into two basic categories: nylon-string and steel-string. As these terms imply, the basic difference lies in the type of strings used. There are also major structural differences. A nylon-string guitar should never be strung with steel strings, and vice versa. For instructions on stringing these guitars, see the following section, "Stringing."

Nylon-String

The nylon-string guitar is commonly used for classical music, soft folk, and certain kinds of jazz and Latin music. Most beginners start with nylon-string guitars because the strings are lighter and easier to fret. The neck of the nylon-string guitar is wide, allowing left-hand fingers more room to move. This type of guitar is also generally less expensive than a steel-string guitar of comparable quality.

Steel-String

The steel-string guitar is well suited to contemporary folk music, bluegrass, country, and blues. This type of guitar is louder than the nylon-string guitar—and can sustain a note longer. This makes the steel-string guitar useful in a band situation either as a rhythm or lead instrument. The neck of the steel-string guitar is generally longer than that of the nylon-string guitar. This makes it easier to play in the higher positions.

Twelve-String

The twelve-string guitar has a full, rich sound that can be heard in many popular venues. This type of guitar has six pairs of strings—and each pair is called a *course*. The lower courses are tuned in octaves. The strings in each of the two highest courses are tuned to the same pitch (in unison). Each course is picked and fretted as if it were one string. Because the twelve-string guitar is more difficult to play than a six-string guitar, it is not usually a good choice for beginners.

The Parts of the Acoustic Guitar

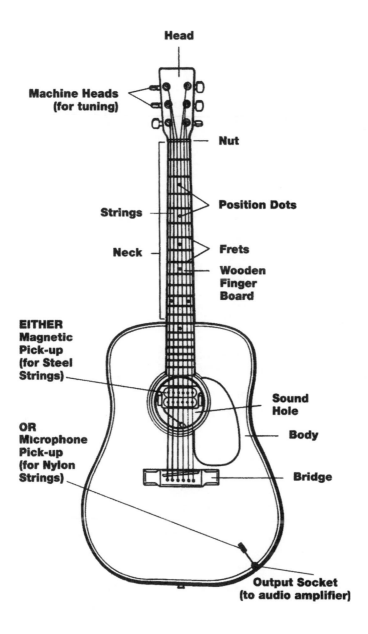

Head

Machine Heads
(for tuning)

Nut

Position Dots

Strings

Frets

Neck

Wooden
Finger
Board

EITHER
Magnetic
Pick-up
(for Steel
Strings)

Sound
Hole

OR
Microphone
Pick-up
(for Nylon
Strings)

Body

Bridge

Output Socket
(to audio amplifier)

Pickups

There are several different types of devices that allow you to electronically amplify an acoustic guitar. For steel-string guitars, there are magnetic pickups similar to those built-in to electric guitars. Various pickups and microphones are also available for nylon-string guitars. Many of today's acoustic guitars come with a built-in pickup system which includes EQ and volume controls, as well as a handy output socket. A microphone-style pickup is shown in the previous diagram.

Acoustic Guitar Comparison: Steel-String and Nylon-String

	Steel-String Guitar	Nylon-String Guitar
Neck	usually 14 frets until joining body	12 frets until joining body
	approximately 1¾ inches wide	approximately 2 inches wide
	usually has a reinforcing steel truss rod	traditionally made without a truss rod
Body	usually slightly bigger than a classical guitar	approximately 19 inches long and 15 inches wide (at the widest point)
Peghead	often has a shield-shaped plastic plate to cover the tip of the truss rod	
	solid peghead with covered or "worm-and-gear" tuning machines	slotted peghead with barrel-type tuning machines
Bridge	has bridge pins or tailpiece to secure strings	strings are tied to bridge

MIDI Guitars

MIDI is an acronym for Musical Instrument Digital Interface (pronounced "middy"). Designed by a world committee, this universal computer language allows MIDI-compatible devices to exchange and store musical information in a precise digital format. At first, MIDI was used primarily for keyboard instruments and sequencers. Now almost any instrument can be set up to send MIDI information. This allows guitarists, wind players, drummers, and even vocalists to control a synthesizer and create a wide variety of musical effects beyond the range of their individual instruments.

Manufacturers offer both acoustic and electric guitars with built-in interfaces. These are both referred to as MIDI guitars. However, any guitar can be retrofitted to send MIDI data using a MIDI pickup.

The first MIDI guitars were not really guitars, but rather MIDI controllers shaped like guitars. With advances in computer music technology, it became possible to build a normal guitar with a special hex pickup to transmit MIDI data. The hex pickup is really six individual pickups—one for each string—in a single unit. Most often, the data is sent in a proprietary format over a special cable to a decoder, which then outputs standard MIDI data that can control a synth. There are also specially designed synths that can accept data directly from the hex pickup. In other systems, the decoder is built in to the guitar, so that the instrument's MIDI output may be plugged directly in to a synth or sequencer.

Specialty Guitars

Stringed instruments have existed for thousands of years— and guitar-like instruments date back at least as far as the Renaissance. Today, there are several related instruments that guitarists find relatively easy to master. These include the tenor guitar, baritone guitar, bass guitar, lap steel, Dobro (or Hawaiian guitar), and ukulele. Instruments in the banjo and mandolin families are closely related to the guitar, and are also easy for the average guitarist to learn quickly.

Electric Guitars

Throughout the 1920s and 1930s, guitarists searched for a way to be heard above the brass and woodwinds of the popular dance band. During this time, acoustic guitarists experimented with microphones and contact pickups. The real breakthrough was the development of the magnetic pickup, which translates the vibration of the guitar's steel strings into an audio signal which can be sent to an amplifier.

Guitar designers realized that an instrument with a magnetic pickup didn't need a large, resonant body to produce sound. They found that a solid-body guitar can actually sustain notes longer than a hollow-body guitar. Thus the modern electric solid-body guitar was born. Hollow-body and semihollow-body electric guitars remain popular to this day due to their distinctive and expressive tonal range.

Although there are literally thousands of different shapes and styles of electric guitar available today, they all share the same basic characteristics shown in the diagram at right.

Solid-Body

The solid-body electric guitar has been the mainstay of rock, pop, R&B, country, and blues music for decades—and it is by far the most popular type of electric guitar used today. All use steel strings and have necks and bodies made of wood, plastic, metal, or composite materials. All have built-in electronics to create an audio signal, an output jack, and volume control. Some have additional features, including active tone control, stereo outputs, multiple pickups, and pickup selector switches.

Hollow-Body

An electric guitar with a resonant, hollow body produces a traditional, warm sound. For this reason, the hollow-body electric guitar is favored by musicians who play jazz, blues, and country swing. Hollow-body electric guitars usually have a carved archtop which gives them a characteristic punchy acoustic sound, even when they are not amplified. When unplugged, the hollow-body electric guitar makes an excellent acoustic guitar.

Semihollow-Body

This type of guitar offers a compromise between the solid-body and hollow-body guitar. Although its body is actually hollow, it is much shallower than a true hollow-body guitar. The semihollow-body guitar still produces some of the warm, resonant sound of the hollow-body guitar. However, the shallower body allows for more sustain and cuts down on inherent feedback problems when playing at high volumes.

The Parts of the Electric Guitar

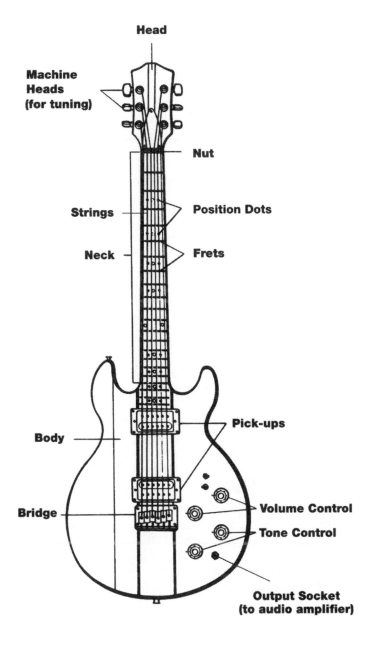

Head

Machine Heads (for tuning)

Nut

Strings

Position Dots

Neck

Frets

Pick-ups

Body

Bridge

Volume Control

Tone Control

Output Socket (to audio amplifier)

Stringing

If you play regularly, you'll probably want to put new strings on your guitar every four to six months. If you play a lot, you may need to change them as often as once a week. In any case, you can tell when you need to restring your guitar by its sound. Old strings can make your tone sound muffled, dead, or even off-pitch. Dirt or rust is also sometimes visible on old steel strings.

If your tone sounds bright and clear, it's not necessary to replace the strings on your guitar. If it sounds dull, it's probably time to change. It's a good idea to keep an extra set of strings in your guitar case so you can replace strings quickly and easily when necessary. If a string breaks, it's probably time to replace the entire set.

Removing Old Strings

Whether you have a nylon-string or steel-string guitar, it's important to remove your old strings with care. Don't be tempted to cut off all the strings at once. Instead, remove them one at a time to protect the neck of your guitar from unnecessary stress. In fact, many guitarists like to replace each string before removing the next. This is probably a good idea with older guitars, as it minimizes the strain put on the neck and body by the string-changing process.

First loosen the tuning peg to release the tension, then cut the string with a scissor (for nylon strings) or wire cutter (for steel strings). Repeat this procedure to remove the remaining strings. Remember that the tips of steel strings can be quite sharp, so take care not to cut yourself when removing these. After you have removed all the old strings, take the time to wipe the fretboard with a clean cloth that is slightly damp. Then wipe off any excess moisture with a dry cloth.

Nylon Strings

As a general rule, nylon strings are all pretty much the same. However, some manufacturers do offer different string tensions. Although the high-tension strings may not necessarily be thicker than low-tension strings, they do have more density. This requires additional string tension, which makes them a bit louder than low-tension strings—and a bit harder to play.

Steel Strings

Steel-string acoustic guitars and electric guitars all require steel strings. These come in different weights called *gauges*. The gauges of the strings affect the relative volume and tone of the sound produced. The thicker the string, the more volume it can produce. Heavy gauge strings are harder to play than light gauge strings. They also put more stress on the neck, bridge, top, and braces of your guitar.

Guitarists often refer to the overall weight of a set of strings in terms of the gauge of the first, or high E, string. Although the gauges of the individual strings in a set vary from one manufacturer to the next, you can get a good idea of the standard gauges available for steel-string acoustic and electric guitars from the following comparison chart. The numbers in parentheses refer to the gauge of the first string in millimeters.

Gauges of Steel Strings

Acoustic Guitar	Electric Guitar
medium (.013)	medium (.011)
light (.012)	light (.009)
extra-light (.010 or .011)	extra-light (.008)

A Word on Stringing

On a standard acoustic guitar, strings are matched to the tuning machines in a circle, from lowest to highest, as shown in the diagram at right.

Here are a few tips to remember when you are stringing an acoustic guitar:

Use the right strings for your instrument: nylon for a nylon-string guitar and steel for a steel-string guitar.

Match each string to the appropriate notches on the bridge and nut.

Don't clip strings to length before putting them on. Tighten them and bring them up to pitch before cutting off any excess.

Avoid putting any kinks or bends in the strings.

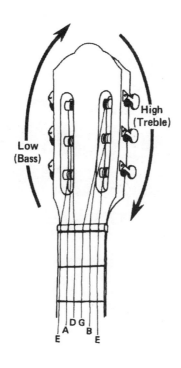

Replacing Nylon Strings

Nylon-string guitars have a simple type of bridge to which the individual strings are tied. Note that some manufacturers produce ball-end nylon strings, which have a small ball or barrel attached to one end of each string. If you have a set of these strings, there is no need to tie the strings to the bridge; just pass the plain end of each string through the appropriate hole in the bridge and skip to the third step.

Insert the end of the string into the proper hole of the bridge and pull it through until about 1 1/2 to 2 inches sticks out the other side. Pass this short end of the string back over the bridge, and then under the main part of the string.

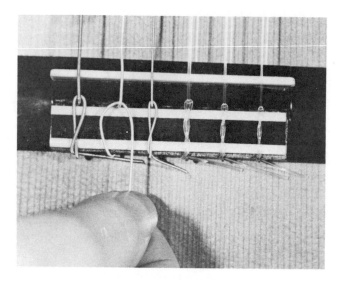

Now pass the short end of the string back over and then under itself to form a loose loop. This loop should resemble a figure eight, as shown below. (For the top three strings, pass the short end of the string over and then under itself a second time to create a double knot.) Then pull gently, but firmly, on the long end of the string to tighten the knot.

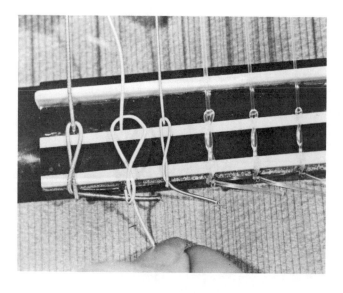

Thread the string through the hole in the tuning-machine barrel from front to rear. Bring the end around the upper side of the barrel and back to the front. Loop the free end around the string as shown at right, and pull it back again.

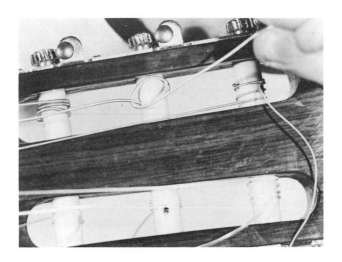

Tune the string until you are sure it won't slip. When the string is tuned up to pitch, there should be at least two full windings on the barrel. Cut both ends of the string fairly short (leave about 1/4 inch) to avoid buzzes and rattles.

Be sure to wind all strings so that the tuning machines turn in the proper direction. As you face the back of the peghead, the tuning pegs should turn counterclockwise for the string to get tighter.

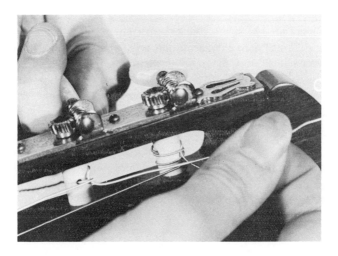

Replacing Steel Strings

On both acoustic and electric guitars the strings are attached to the machine heads on one end and to the bridge at the other. When restringing your guitar, you should always be careful to avoid getting any bends or kinks in the new strings. Take care when uncoiling and handling the new strings, as the tips can be very sharp.

Acoustic and electric steel-string guitars are all pretty much the same at the headstock end, but there are several variations on the way that the strings are attached to the instrument's other end. Most acoustic steel-string guitars have a bridge with bridge pins. If your guitar has a row of small plastic pins along the bridge, you can skip ahead to the section "Replacing Strings on a Guitar with Bridge Pins." If your guitar has a tailpiece, read the following paragraphs and then skip to the instructions on the adjacent page.

Restringing a Tailpiece Guitar

All solid-body electric guitars and some acoustic guitars have some type of tailpiece bridge. On acoustic guitars, the tailpiece is often anchored to the strap button at the bottom of the instrument. This type of tailpiece is called a *trapeze tailpiece.* There are many other varieties of tailpiece-type bridges, including *stop-tailpieces, tremolo bridges, locking-tremolo bridges,* and so on.

With some tailpiece bridges, the ball end of the string fits into a notch in the tailpiece. With other types, you must pass the string up through a hole in the body of the guitar. Certain high-tech tremolo bridges may require the use of a special tool to remove and replace the strings. Before removing any strings, examine carefully how they are attached to your particular type of tailpiece. Remove and replace strings one at a time, so that you will always have a model to copy.

Restringing a Guitar with Bridge Pins

To get the old string off, loosen it completely, then gently push it back into its hole. At this point you should be able to remove the bridge pin. If you have trouble getting the pin out, you can use a screwdriver or a coin to gently pry it loose. Just be sure to use an adjacent bridge pin as a fulcrum, rather than the bridge itself, to avoid damaging the wood.

Put the ball end of the new string into the correct hole. Insert the bridge pin so that the grooved side faces the string. The slot and the tension created by tuning will be enough to secure the string. For now, tug gently on the long end of the string to make sure that it is snugly in place.

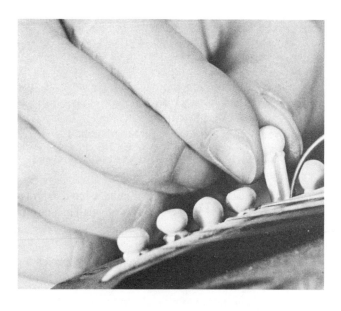

Thread the string straight through the hole in the appropriate tuning-machine post at the head of the guitar. Gently bring the free end halfway around the post: clockwise for the bass strings and counterclockwise for the treble strings.

Loop the free end of the string under the longer part and bend it back gently. As the string is tightened, this loop will lock it in place and prevent it from slipping. When the string is in tune, there should be at least one winding around the post. Cut this end of the string fairly short (leave about 1/4 inch) to avoid buzzes and rattles.

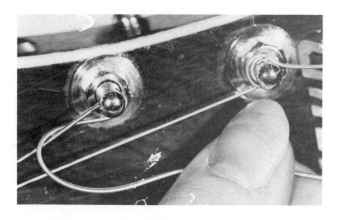

TUNING

Whether you're playing a gig or practicing at home, you will always sound your best when your instrument is well tuned. In a group setting, it's important that musicians can tune quickly and accurately—and maintain good tuning throughout the session. This section provides complete instructions on tuning your guitar using three common methods.

You can find alternate tunings and chords in the section "Open Tunings" in *Book 4: Guitar Chord Dictionary.*

Relative Tuning

If your guitar is already pretty well in tune, you can use the relative tuning method to tune up. You can tune each string of the guitar to its correct pitch by turning the appropriate tuning peg.

*   Use a left-hand finger to press down on the sixth string (low E) just behind (to the left of) the fifth fret. When you pluck this string, you will hear an A note. This note should sound the same as the fifth string played open (that is, without being fretted by a left-hand finger).

*   If the fifth string (or A string) does not sound in tune, use the tuning peg to loosen it until it sounds lower than the sixth string, fifth fret. Then slowly bring it up to pitch.

*   When your A string is in tune, fret it at the fifth fret. This note is D, and should sound the same as the open D, or fourth, string.

*   When your D string is in tune, fret it at the fifth fret. This note is G, and should sound the same as the open G, or third, string.

*   When your G string is in tune, fret it at the fourth fret. This note is B, and should sound the same as the open B, or second, string.

*   When your B string is in tune, fret it at the fifth fret. This note is E, and should sound the same as the open high E, or first, string.

This diagram summarizes the relative tuning method.

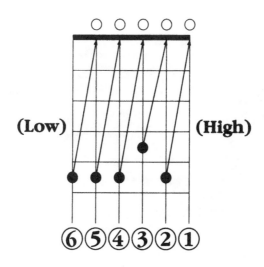

Tuning by Harmonics

Harmonics are tones produced without actually fretting a string. The easiest harmonics to sound are those produced by touching the strings at the twelfth fret.

To play harmonics, just touch a string lightly with a left-hand finger directly above the fret indicated. Then pluck the string with your right-hand index or middle finger and remove the left-hand finger from the string immediately. The result is a high, bell-like tone. For this reason, harmonics are often referred to as *chimes*.

Like the relative tuning method, this method can only help you get your guitar in tune to itself. If you are playing with other people, you will need to need to tune at least one of your strings to one of the other instruments before applying this tuning method.

* Assuming that your low E (sixth) string is in tune, sound the harmonic at the fifth fret. This tone (E) should sound the same as the harmonic on the A (fifth) string, seventh fret. If the two tones are not perfectly in tune, loosen the A string until it sounds lower, and then slowly bring it up to pitch.

* When your A string is in tune, sound its harmonic at the fifth fret. Compare and match this tone (A) to the harmonic on the D (fourth) string, seventh fret.

* When your D string is in tune, sound its harmonic at the fifth fret. Compare and match this tone (D) to the harmonic on the G (third) string, seventh fret.

* To tune the B (second) string, sound the harmonic at the seventh fret of the low E (sixth) string. Compare and match this tone (B) to the open B (second) string.

* To tune the high E (first) string, sound the harmonic at the fifth fret of the low E (sixth) string. Compare and match this tone (E) to the open high E (first) string.

Tuning to a Piano

You can use a piano or electronic keyboard instrument to tune each string of your guitar. If you are tuning to an acoustic piano, it's naturally important that the piano itself is well tuned.

Here are the notes on the keyboard that correspond to the open strings of the guitar. These notes represent the actual sounds of the guitar strings. Music for guitar is written one octave higher than it sounds to make it easier to read.

Tuning to a Piano

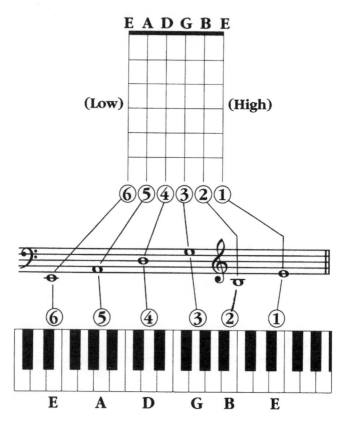

Maintenance

Most guitars don't require much in the way of special care. In fact, if you treat it right, a good guitar should last a lifetime. In this section, you will find some valuable advice on maintaining your instrument, some tips on storage and travel, and an overview of the most common guitar repairs. There are also descriptions of popular guitar accessories that can help extend the life of your instrument or make it easier to play.

Cases

Like other instruments, the guitar should always be stored and transported in a case. The least expensive case is a plastic cover with a zipper known as a *gig bag*. This type of case will protect your instrument from dirt and moisture—and prevent most nicks and scratches. However, they offer little real protection against bangs and bumps which may occur during travel. *Cardboard* cases offer more protection and additional space to carry accessories. There are also high-quality, padded gig bags made of leather, canvas, or nylon which offer a significantly higher level of protection than the simple plastic variety.

Semi-hardshell cases are made from thin wood or fiberboard. This shell is covered with high-grade vinyl, and occasionally there is padding between the wood and the vinyl cover. The inside is usually lined with a soft material, allowing the guitar to rest snugly and not bang around while it is being carried.

Hardshell cases are similar to the semi-hardshell. The hardshell case is made from thicker wood (usually fi-inch plywood) and thus offers more protection. Moreover, the inside is often more thickly padded than the semi-hardshell case. Although the hardshell case offers more than adequate protection under almost any circumstances, its main drawback is that it is heavy. Some companies make *fiberglass* cases which are extremely protective, but weigh comparatively less. As the quality of the case increases, so does the quality of the hardware (latches, hinges, and handles). Most cases have one latch that locks. While this lock cannot prevent theft, it can discourage the uninvited borrower.

No matter what kind of case you have, make sure that your guitar fits snugly inside. Rattling around in a case that fits loosely can at least knock a guitar out of tune, and may eventually lead to more serious problems. If you cannot find a case that is a perfect fit for your instrument, use a towel or a clean, soft rag for padding.

At home, many guitarists like to leave their instrument out of the case. Don't invite a costly fall by leaning your instrument up against the furniture or wall. Instead, purchase a guitar stand to keep your instrument safe, yet accessible.

Travel

If you travel a lot with your guitar, you should use a hardshell or semi-hardshell case. This should protect your instrument from the inevitable dings and cracks that can occur during transit. If you are traveling by car, don't leave your guitar in the trunk for extended periods of time. In summer, the trunk can heat up like an oven. In winter, the trunk can expose an instrument to excessive cold. When you bring a guitar in from the cold, let it warm up gradually in the case for twenty minutes or so before taking it out and playing.

The baggage compartment of an airplane is subject to changes in temperature and air pressure that can damage your instrument. Before traveling by plane, loosen all the strings of your guitar until they sag. You might want to consider insuring your instrument. It is not advisable to check an expensive guitar as baggage.

Storage

A guitar is basically made of wood and glue, so anything that can damage these materials can damage your instrument. Avoid storing your guitar in any extremes of heat, cold, dryness, and/or moisture. If you plan to store your guitar for several months, you should probably first loosen all the strings until they sag.

If you live where there is central heating in winter, beware of dryness. Keep an eye out for gaps in the bridge or neck, and consider buying a humidifier. Immediately wipe off any perspiration or moisture from the guitar. Use a soft, clean cloth and rub gently with the grain.

Nicks and scratches on the surface of your guitar do not affect the sound of the instrument. However, they can affect the resale value. Expensive guitars can be insured, usually in a rider to an existing homeowner's insurance policy.

Cleaning

You should clean and polish your guitar periodically. This improves the physical beauty of the instrument and helps to preserve and protect its wood finish. Use lemon oil, boiled linseed oil, or guitar polish. You may wish to use a polish made or endorsed by the company that makes your guitar.

Use a soft, damp cloth to polish your guitar. For a thorough job, take off the strings and rub down the neck as well. This will get rid of the buildup of dirt and oil that can accumulate, and may even affect intonation. Don't use commercial furniture polishes with silicones or other synthetic additives. These may dull or even ruin your instrument's finish. Be sure to wipe off excess polish or oil with a clean cloth.

Lubrication

You should periodically lubricate open tuning machines (called *worm-and-gear*). Put a small amount of petroleum jelly on the end of a toothpick, and insert it in the gears. Use very little lubricant, and wipe off any excess which may attract dust and dirt.

REPAIR

If your instrument starts to rattle or buzz when you play it, or if it won't stay in tune, or if it sounds out of tune when you play at certain positions up the neck, it may be in need of some repair. Repairs to the body and neck of a guitar are best left to the professional repairperson. Still, it is a good idea to be familiar with the causes of these problems so that you can talk intelligently with whomever you choose to entrust your instrument to. In addition to getting an estimate before agreeing to let someone work on your guitar, be sure that you understand specifically what the repairperson intends to do to the instrument. Do not be afraid to ask questions. If someone tells you something that doesn't sound quite right, don't hesitate to get a second opinion.

Initially, whatever repairs you are likely to need will be simple ones—easily affordable and easily accomplished by the staff of your local music store. As you gain more experience (and your instrument gets older), you may realize the need for more extensive repairs or adjustments. Keep in mind that the cost of a major repair—such as refretting or resetting the neck—may actually exceed the value of the instrument. At this point you may find it more prudent to invest in a better guitar.

What follows is an overview of the most common guitar-repair situations. Some of these problems you can fix yourself with standard household tools if you are fairly handy. At any rate, you will find some valuable tips to help you determine just what is wrong with your guitar before you take it in to the shop.

The Frets

If you hear a buzz when you play your instrument, it may be because it has a loose fret. Check each fret, one by one, by pressing one end of the fret down with your finger and then letting go to see if there is any movement. Do this on both sides of the fret. Since you sometimes have to press quite hard, you might want to use the point of a pliers (or similar instrument that is not too sharp). Be careful not to damage the fretboard as you check for loose frets.

If you find a loose fret, you can repair it yourself pretty easily. First place your guitar on its side so that the loose end of the fret is on top. Now press the loose end to the fingerboard with your plier point and let one drop of cyanoacrylate "super glue" run down between the fret and board. Press the fret down for a few minutes while the glue dries. If you get any glue on your skin or tools, you can remove it using acetone (nail polish remover). Never apply acetone to your guitar, as it will dissolve the finish. If you do get glue on the side of the fingerboard, you can sand it off using very fine (600 grit) sandpaper.

If none of your frets are loose, but you still hear string buzzes, this may mean that some of the frets are worn or uneven. In this case the frets must be dressed, or filed to make them even. In extreme cases, as with older guitars that have seen a lot of use, it may be necessary to replace the frets.

The Tuning Machines

If you hear a rattling noise when you play your guitar, it may originate from the tuning machines. First check that the small setscrews in the ends of the pegs are not loose. Note that over-tightening this screw may make the peg difficult or impossible to turn; just tighten them until they are snug to avoid rattles. The next parts to check are the nuts that go over the tuning peg on the face of the peghead. These may be tightened with a standard pair of pliers, taking care not to scratch the peghead. If all of the setscrews and peg nuts are tight, check the small screws on the back of the peghead that fasten the machines to the peghead. Take care not to over-tighten these screws, because if you strip the screwholes you will worsen the very problem you are trying to remedy.

Another cause of rattling is loose string ends vibrating against the peghead. This is easily fixed by snipping off the excess with a pair of wire cutters. On classical guitars, also check the bridge ends of the strings to make sure that they are not vibrating against the face.

The Neck

It's very important that the neck of your guitar is in good condition and that it is properly fused to the body. To check for a loose neck, first grab the neck of the guitar near the heel (base) and grab the body of the guitar with the other hand. Then twist your hands in opposite directions to see if there is any movement at the joint. If so, the neck should be repaired. With electric Fenders and other guitars with bolt-on necks, this problem can be easily fixed. However, a loose neck is a major repair for an acoustic guitar, and can be rather expensive. A guitar with a warped (twisted) neck is almost impossible to repair satisfactorily.

To check the straightness of your guitar's neck, first loosen all the strings. Then place the guitar on a table and lay a straightedge lengthwise along the neck to determine if it has a concave or convex bow. If the neck is bowed, you may be able to correct it by adjusting the truss rod (see below). If your guitar doesn't have a truss rod, you will have to take it to a professional repairperson for a "heatset," in which the neck is heated and clamped to correct the bow.

If the neck is straight, the next thing to check is whether it is set properly in relation to the body. On some electric guitars with glued-on necks, the neck should slant back at about a five-degree angle in relation to the face of the guitar. On acoustic guitars and electric guitars with bolt-on necks, the neck should be parallel to the face of the guitar. Sight down the fingerboard (not the tops of the frets) from the peghead end. If the neck is attached at the proper angle, your sightline should hit the bridge about one or two millimeters (0.04 to 0.05 inches) below its top. (This distance may be a bit more on classical guitars.) If this distance is more than two millimeters, the neck may have to be reset. This is easily accomplished on a guitar with a bolt-on neck by using a shim made of wood, plastic, or cardboard. On a guitar with a glued-on neck, such as most acoustic guitars, this may be a very involved repair or may not be possible at all.

A *truss rod* is a steel rod put in the neck for reinforcement. It does not adjust the angle of how the neck is fixed to the guitar body. The truss rod can only straighten the neck between the nut and the twelfth or fourteenth fret. Necks that have an adjustable truss rod have a nut screwed on a rod sticking out on one end of the neck. Most often you will find this in the headstock under a little cover plate (for instance, on Gibson guitars). You may also find it on the other end of the neck, as in the case of many Fender guitars. On some acoustic guitars, the truss rod nut is located inside the body and must be accessed through the sound hole.

A neck with a concave bend may be corrected by turning the truss rod nut clockwise using the proper wrench. For a convex neck, turn the nut counterclockwise. Check your straight-edge after every quarter turn to determine if the neck is straight. Unless you are absolutely sure what you are doing, you should never turn the truss-rod nut more than half or three-quarters of a turn in either direction. Over-tightening or over-loosening the truss-rod adjustment could cause serious damage to the instrument.

The Finish

Many of the less expensive guitars have a polyurethane finish. This can be a problem if you want to do a touch-up job, since the new finish won't blend in with the old. In this event, even the most expert touch-up will reveal a "ghost line" at best. You won't have that problem with guitars that have the conventional lacquer finishes. New lacquer will blend invisibly with old lacquer. If you do not have much experience refinishing instruments, you should probably leave this job to the professionals.

The Body

It's important that an acoustic guitar has a perfectly straight top. Check to see that the top is not slightly swollen behind the bridge. If it is swollen, the chances are good that it is concave in front of the bridge. If this is the case, it could be that one or more braces or the bridge plate is loose. To check for this, take a small inspection mirror and a flashlight and look through the sound hole at the braces and bridge plate as you press down firmly on the swollen top. If the braces move, the swell can probably be corrected by professional regluing. If you cannot locate a loose brace or bridge plate, then it's possible that the guitar is not repairable.

Cracks and warping in the body of the guitar must be corrected by a professional, which can be rather expensive. Be sure to compare the cost of such a repair to the cost of purchasing a new instrument of similar or better quality.

Accessories

There are dozens of accessories available to the guitarist. These may increase the versatility of the instrument or make it easier to maintain or play. The most common accessories are listed below. To learn more about other guitar accessories or keep abreast of new products, periodically browse music supply catalogs and music stores.

Capos

A capo fits over the neck of the guitar and presses down on the strings at any fret. In this way, it allows the guitarist to change keys without learning a complete set of new chord forms. Capos come in a number of different styles. Although the all-metal spring-type capo is preferred for its strength, some guitarists feel they scratch the back of the guitar's neck. The most common capo is the elastic-band type. A single-band capo is used for a nylon-string guitar, while a double-band capo is used for the steel-string guitar.

Humidifiers

Many nylon-string guitarists use a portable humidifier to protect their instruments from dryness, particularly during the winter. (Humidifiers are not recommended for steel-string guitars, as external humidity will cause the strings to rust.) The humidifier can prevent cracking and warping brought on by indoor heating or a desert climate. A commercial guitar humidifier is basically a sponge in a rubber sheath which clips on to the sound hole. This comes with a color-coded card that gauges the humidity. If you would prefer to make your own guitar humidifier, first take a small plastic container or sturdy plastic bag and perforate the top with small holes. Insert a slightly damp sponge and keep it in your case. Occasionally check the sponge to ensure that it is not too dry or damp.

Peg Winders

If you change strings frequently, this inexpensive accessory is an invaluable tool. One end of the peg winder is a hollow cup that fits over the tuning peg. The other end is a handle. Together they form a crank that makes the job of winding and unwinding strings considerably easier and quicker.

Tuning Aids

There are several accessories available that help the guitarist tune with speed and accuracy. The tuning fork provides a single tone to start off the tuning process. An E or A tuning fork is best for tuning the standard guitar. The pitch pipe provides all tones in the chromatic scale. Electronic tuners are the most expensive of all tuning aids. These not only provide any desired pitch, they also evaluate the pitch you play and indicate whether or not it is in tune.

Picks

Picks are an important accessory for many steel-string guitarists who play rock, folk, bluegrass, blues, or jazz. There are basically two types of picks: flatpicks and fingerpicks. The most common type of flatpick is a plastic triangle with rounded edges. This type of pick comes in three different thicknesses: light, medium, and heavy. Generally speaking, the lighter-weight picks are used for single melody-line (lead) playing, while heavy picks are reserved for rhythm.

Fingerpicks are used by folk and old-time blues guitarists who play in the fingerpicking style. If you would like to explore this style, use a plastic thumbpick and three metal fingerpicks. The fingerpicks should be put on so the metal curves with the pad of your finger. Some guitarists prefer to use only a thumbpick to take advantage of the rich bass sound it produces.

Straps

If you perform in public, it's a good idea to have a guitar strap. This accessory allows the guitarist to stand and move about the stage with ease. These come in a wide range of colors, styles, and prices. In order to put a strap on your guitar, the instrument must have at least one strap button at the very bottom of its body. The other end of the strap may either be attached to another strap button near the neck of the guitar or tied to the peghead, above the nut and under the strings.

Most nylon-string guitars are made without strap buttons. There are special straps that go around the bottom of the guitar and hook into the sound hole to support the instrument. This kind of strap is adequate for occasional use—but if you want to play standing up on a regular basis, get a professional repairperson to install strap buttons and use a conventional guitar strap.

Stands

If you like to leave your guitar out of its case and ready to play, you should definitely get a guitar stand. This accessory is also important if you play more than one instrument in performance. Guitar stands are usually made of metal and allow you to stand the guitar upright with the neck pointing upward.

If you use printed music or charts when you practice or perform, you should also consider buying a music stand. If you plan to travel, make sure you consider the portability of the stands you choose. Both guitar and music stands are available in light collapsible models that are easy to transport and store. If you plan to use your stand at home, you may want to get a sturdier model that does not collapse. Both guitar and music stands are available in a wide range of prices.

2

Music Theory for Guitarists

Your continued study of the mechanics of music will help you to focus on the art of creating it. This book provides a solid introduction to music theory—the study of how musical sounds interrelate melodically, harmonically, and rhythmically. There's also a useful section on tablature and other notation used especially for guitar music.

To learn more about the practical applications of music theory for the guitarist, see "Scale Basics" in *Book 3: Guitar Scale Dictionary* and "Basic Chord Theory" in *Book 4: Guitar Chord Dictionary.*

READING MUSIC

The sections that follow provide basic information on reading standard music notation. Many of these concepts are also important when it comes to reading guitar tablature which is covered later in the book.

Notes on the Staff

Written music is a universal language of notes and symbols, arranged on the musical *staff*, which consists of five lines and four spaces.

The Treble Clef

Clefs are symbols that provide a frame of reference for writing notes on the staff. In other words, the clef tells the musician exactly which tones are indicated by the notes occurring on each line and space of the staff.

There are two clefs that commonly appear in written music: the *treble clef* and the *bass clef*. The treble clef is usually used in music intended for middle- and high-range instruments and voices, while the bass clef is used in music written for lower instruments and voices. Let's take a look at the treble clef on the staff.

This clef is also sometimes called the *G clef* because the curlicue of the clef sign circles the second line up from the bottom of the staff. This line marks the position of the G note, and so provides a frame of reference for notes placed on any of the other lines and spaces of the staff.

Naming Notes

Notes are the building blocks of music. Each note usually indicates two qualities: pitch and duration. *Pitch* is simply how high or low a particular tone sounds. *Duration* is how long an individual tone should last. We'll get into note duration in the next chapter. For now, let's focus on how notes indicate pitch.

Musical notes are named using the first seven letters of the alphabet: A, B, C, D, E, F, and G. These letter names indicate notes in an ascending sequence—from low to high. After the final G note, the sequence begins again: A, B, C, D, E, F, G; A, B, C, D, E, F, G; and so on. Most instruments are able to produce a large enough range of notes to repeat this seven-note sequence several times.

The distance between any two notes with the same letter name is called an *octave*. This term, from the Greek word meaning "eight," reminds us that a note's letter name repeats at every eighth tone of the sequence. Although the two tones that form an octave are actually different notes, each tone sounds as if it were just a higher or lower version of the same note.

The Staff

Here are some notes arranged on the staff in the treble clef. Notice that a note falls on every line and space of the staff.

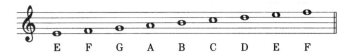

Take the time to memorize the position and name of each of these notes.

Leger Lines

Now that you are familiar with the notes on the staff in the treble clef, take a look at the notes that extend above and below the staff. The additional lines used to extend notes beyond the staff in this way are referred to as *leger lines*.

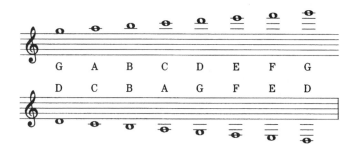

The Bass Clef

Now take a look at the notes in the bass clef. This clef is also sometimes called the *F clef* because it forms a curlicue on the fourth line up from the bottom of the staff. Thus, the F note serves as a reference point for all other notes on the staff. This clef is used to notate music for the bass guitar.

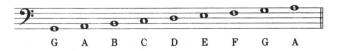

Take the time to memorize the position and name of each of these bass clef notes.

Note Values and Rhythm

As you have learned, the position of the note on the staff indicates a particular *pitch* (that is, how high or low a note sounds). Each note also has a *note value*, or *duration*, (that is, how long the note should last). The duration of a note is counted in beats. Here are the basic note shapes and their usual durations. Take the time to memorize the appearance and value of each of these notes.

꣠ A **whole note** lasts four beats

♩ A **half note** lasts two beats

♩ A **quarter note** lasts one beat

♪ An **eighth note** lasts one-half beat

♪ A **sixteenth note** lasts one-fourth beat

♪ A **thirty-second note** lasts one-eighth beat.

An eighth note has three components. The circular portion of the note is called the *notehead*, the line is called the *stem*, and the tail at the top is called the *flag*.

Stem →♪← Flag
←Head

The flag of the sixteenth note is made with two lines, while the thirty-second-note flag is made of three lines. Groups of consecutive eighth, sixteenth, and thirty-second notes are often linked with *beams*, as shown.

Eighth Notes   Sixteenth Notes   Thirty-second Notes

Stem direction is determined by a note's placement on the staff. In either clef, notes occurring below the middle line of the staff have stems that point upward. Notes that occur on or above the middle line should have downward stems. Although this is the preferable rule regarding stem direction, some printed music features notes on the middle line with upward stems. These occur only when other notes in the same measure feature upward stems. Notes connected by a beam should always feature the same stem direction (as determined by the natural stem direction of the majority of notes in the group).

Compare the different notes you have learned and their relative values.

Whole Note:

Half Note:

Quarter Note:

Eighth Note:

Sixteenth Note:

Thirty-second Note:

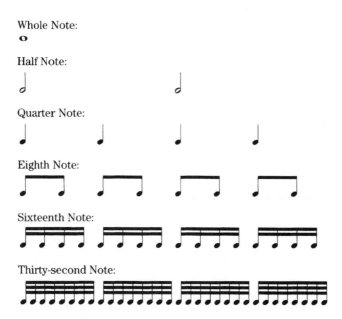

As you can see, two half-notes equal the duration of one whole-note, four quarter-notes equal the duration of one whole-note, eight eighth-notes equal the duration of one whole-note, and so on.

In order to make it easy to count the rhythm of written music, the staff is divided into sections called *measures*, or *bars*. The vertical lines that divide the staff in this way are called *barlines*. A *double barline* is used to indicate the end of a piece of music. (A lighter double barline is used to divide important sections of a piece.)

Take a look at some of the different note values in measures on the staff. Each measure in this example contains four beats. Count the beats of each measure aloud slowly and evenly while you clap the rhythm indicated by the notes.

Count: 1 2 3 4   1 2 3 4   1 2 3 and 4 and

The next example combines notes of different durations in each measure. Count the beats aloud as you clap the indicated rhythm. Again, be sure to count slowly and evenly without halting.

Count: 1 2 3 4 1 2 and 3 4   1 and 2 3 4

Now that you are familiar with these basic note values, get ready to combine your knowledge of pitch and rhythm to read a familiar song melody. First count and clap the rhythm of "Jingle Bells." Then play or sing the melody slowly and evenly.

Jingle Bells

Rests

Music is usually composed of sounds and silences. The silent beats in music are represented by signs called *rests*. Rests are named and valued like the note values you learned in the previous section.

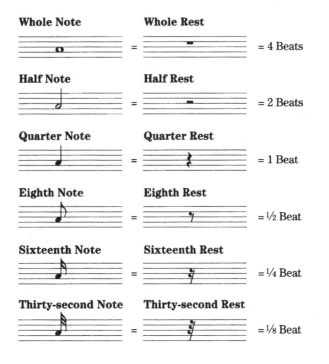

Whole Note	Whole Rest	
𝅝	= —	= 4 Beats
Half Note	**Half Rest**	
𝅗𝅥	= ▬	= 2 Beats
Quarter Note	**Quarter Rest**	
♩	= 𝄽	= 1 Beat
Eighth Note	**Eighth Rest**	
♪	= 𝄾	= ½ Beat
Sixteenth Note	**Sixteenth Rest**	
𝅘𝅥𝅯	= 𝄿	= ¼ Beat
Thirty-second Note	**Thirty-second Rest**	
𝅘𝅥𝅰	= 𝅀	= ⅛ Beat

Notes and Rests

Notes and rests may be combined in the same measure, as long as their combined values add up to the correct number of beats (in this example, four beats to a measure). Count the beats of this phrase as you clap the rhythm of the notes.

Count the beats of this next phrase as you clap the rhythm of the notes. Now play or sing this melody slowly and evenly.

Pickup Notes

Certain song melodies require an incomplete first measure to provide for a *pickup*, which is simply a note or notes that occur before the first stressed beat of the song. When a musical composition features a partial measure containing a pickup, it usually makes up the remaining beats of the first measure in the last measure of the piece. This means that the last measure of the piece will also be incomplete. You can see how this works in "Polly-Wolly Doodle."

Polly-Wolly Doodle

Dotted Notes and Rests

A dot placed after any note or rest means that it should last one-and-a-half times its normal duration. For example, if you add a dot after a half note (which normally lasts two beats), you get a *dotted half note*, which has a duration of three beats.

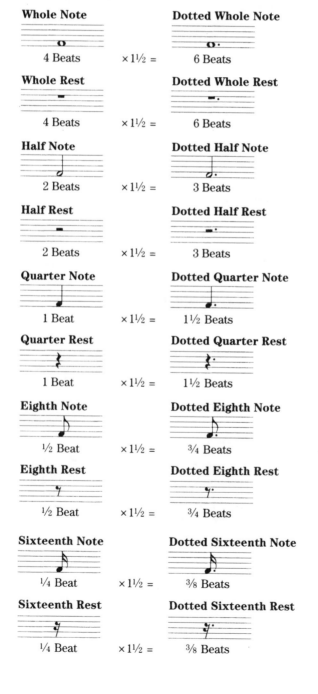

It's easy to understand dotted notes and rests when you compare them with the regular note and rest values you have already learned.

Whole Note		Dotted Whole Note
4 Beats	$\times 1\frac{1}{2} =$	6 Beats
Whole Rest		**Dotted Whole Rest**
4 Beats	$\times 1\frac{1}{2} =$	6 Beats
Half Note		**Dotted Half Note**
2 Beats	$\times 1\frac{1}{2} =$	3 Beats
Half Rest		**Dotted Half Rest**
2 Beats	$\times 1\frac{1}{2} =$	3 Beats
Quarter Note		**Dotted Quarter Note**
1 Beat	$\times 1\frac{1}{2} =$	$1\frac{1}{2}$ Beats
Quarter Rest		**Dotted Quarter Rest**
1 Beat	$\times 1\frac{1}{2} =$	$1\frac{1}{2}$ Beats
Eighth Note		**Dotted Eighth Note**
$\frac{1}{2}$ Beat	$\times 1\frac{1}{2} =$	$\frac{3}{4}$ Beats
Eighth Rest		**Dotted Eighth Rest**
$\frac{1}{2}$ Beat	$\times 1\frac{1}{2} =$	$\frac{3}{4}$ Beats
Sixteenth Note		**Dotted Sixteenth Note**
$\frac{1}{4}$ Beat	$\times 1\frac{1}{2} =$	$\frac{3}{8}$ Beats
Sixteenth Rest		**Dotted Sixteenth Rest**
$\frac{1}{4}$ Beat	$\times 1\frac{1}{2} =$	$\frac{3}{8}$ Beats

Thirty-second Note	**Dotted Thirty-second Note**
⅛ Beat × 1½ =	³⁄₁₆ Beats
Thirty-second Rest	**Dotted Thirty-second Rest**
⅛ Beat × 1½ =	³⁄₁₆ Beats

Take the time to memorize the appearance and value of each dotted note and rest. Then count the beats in the next example as you clap the rhythm indicated by the notes. (Notice how the dotted eighth notes are connected by beams to the sixteenth notes in the third measure.)

Now combine your knowledge of pitch and rhythm as you play or sing the opening phrase of "I've Been Working on the Railroad."

I've Been Working on the Railroad

You may also encounter a *double dotted note* in written music. Two dots indicate that the note is worth one and three-fourths of its normal value. In this way, a double dotted whole note lasts for seven beats. A double dotted half note lasts for three-and-a-half beats.

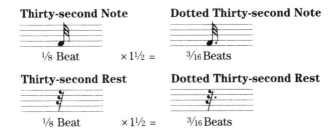

Time Signatures

Every musical composition has a *time signature* at the beginning of the first staff. This symbol indicates two important facts about the overall rhythm of the piece.

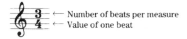 ← Number of beats per measure
← Value of one beat

The top number of the time signature indicates how many beats there are in each measure. The bottom number determines which type of note is worth one beat.

2 = Half Note
4 = Quarter Note
8 = Eighth Note

The time signature is a guidepost to the overall rhythm of a piece of music. Each time signature also has a characteristic pattern of stressed and unstressed beats. In the sections that follow, you'll take a look at some basic time signatures and their characteristic patterns of stress.

⁴⁄₄ *Time*

⁴⁄₄ (pronounced "four-four") is the most common time signature used in written music. Much of the music we've examined in the book so far has been in ⁴⁄₄ time—with four beats in each measure and the quarter note lasting for its natural value of one beat. The ⁴⁄₄ time signature is so prevalent that it is sometimes referred to as "common time" and notated with a "**C**" symbol, as shown.

← 4 beats per measure
← A quarter note gets one beat

Each time signature has a natural, characteristic pattern of stressed and unstressed beats. The first beat of each measure in any time signature receives the most stress. In ⁴⁄₄ time, the third beat is also stressed, but to a lesser extent. "Jingle Bells" provides a strong example of the natural stresses that occur in ⁴⁄₄ time. (The stressed beats are indicated with boldface numbers.)

Jingle Bells

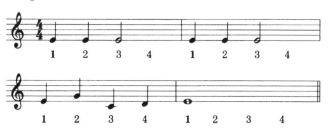

$\frac{3}{4}$ *Time*

$\frac{3}{4}$ (or "three-four") time is also sometimes called *waltz time*, since this is the characteristic time signature of this dance form. However, there are many other types of compositions that employ this time signature. In $\frac{3}{4}$ time, the quarter note still receives its normal value, but there are only three beats in every measure.

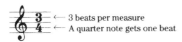
← 3 beats per measure
← A quarter note gets one beat

The natural stress of $\frac{3}{4}$ time falls on the first beat of each measure only. Sing or hum the first phrase of "Drink to Me Only with Thine Eyes" to get a feeling for the lilting stress of $\frac{3}{4}$ time.

Drink to Me Only with Thine Eyes

$\frac{2}{4}$ *Time*

$\frac{2}{4}$ time calls for only two beats in each measure with a stress on every other beat. Richard Wagner's familiar "Wedding March" illustrates the strong and regular stress pattern of this time signature. Notice the bass clef.

Wedding March

$\frac{2}{2}$ *Time*

$\frac{2}{2}$ time, or *cut time*, indicates that a half note lasts for only one beat—with two beats in each measure. $\frac{2}{2}$ time is usually noted with this shorthand symbol (¢). This time signature makes it easier for musicians to read music with many short note values or complex rhythms. Here's the traditional fiddle tune "Turkey in the Straw" in $\frac{2}{2}$ time. Notice that the stresses fall on every other beat.

Turkey in the Straw

$\frac{3}{2}$ *and* $\frac{4}{2}$ *Time*

$\frac{3}{2}$ and $\frac{4}{2}$ time signatures also call for the half note to equal one beat.

$\frac{2}{8}$, $\frac{3}{8}$, *and* $\frac{4}{8}$ *Time*

Some time signatures call for an eighth note to be valued as one beat. Try counting aloud as you clap the rhythm of these phrases. (Stressed beats are indicated with bold-face numbers.)

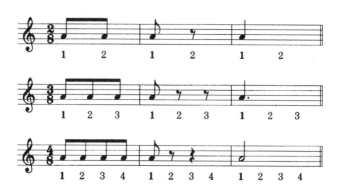

All of the time signatures we've looked at so far are called *simple time signatures* because they require a basic arrangement of the number of beats in each measure and the value of each beat. *Compound time signatures* will be discussed in a later section.

Accidentals

Sharp, flat, and *natural notes* are collectively called *accidentals.* These notes are formed by adding a *sharp sign* (♯), *flat sign* (♭), or *natural sign* (♮) before the note.

Sharps

Here's the complete sequence of natural and sharp note names.

A-A♯-B-C-C♯-D-D♯-E-F-F♯-G-G♯-A

The distance between each of these notes is called a *half step.* Notice that no sharp occurs between the E and F keys, or between the B and C keys.

Flats

Here's the complete sequence of natural and flat note names.

A-B♭-B-C-D♭-D-E♭-E-F-G♭-G-A♭-A

If a note appears with a sharp or flat sign, all subsequent notes in the same position on the staff of that measure are also affected by that sign. Note that the barline cancels both sharp and flat signs.

Naturals

A *natural sign* is placed before a note to cancel a sharp or flat sign used previously with that note. Once a natural sign has been used, all subsequent notes in the same position on the staff in that measure are natural.

A natural sign may be canceled by a flat or sharp sign. (Notice that the barline then cancels the sharp.)

Some pieces contain both sharps and flats. As a general rule, an accidental that leads up to a natural note is written as a sharp note—and an accidental that leads down to a natural note is written as a flat note. This rule is illustrated in "Melancholy Baby."

Melancholy Baby

Major Keys and Scales

So far, we've looked at sharp, flat, and natural notes that are individually added to written music. These notes are called *accidentals* or *altered notes.* Many pieces of music require that certain notes be sharped or flatted as a general rule. The number of sharps or flats that occur regularly in a piece of music determines the key. Rather than writing in a sharp or flat sign every time one should occur, these signs are written in a *key signature* at the beginning of each staff.

Composers and arrangers place music in different keys to accommodate the needs of the particular ranges of the voices or instruments for which they are writing. Certain keys are easier to play on certain instruments. Using different keys for the individual sections or songs in a larger work—such as a symphony or a Broadway show—adds variety to a performance. This is important to remember if you are planning your own concert, or writing music for others to perform.

The Key of C Major

Most of the musical examples in the book so far have been written in the *key of C major,* which has no sharps or flats. Thus, all the notes of the C major scale occur on the white keys of the piano keyboard. Once you understand the construction of the scale in the key of C major, you'll be able to build the scale and key signature for every other major key.

As you already know, the shortest distance between two notes, is called a half step. A *whole step* is the equivalent of two half-steps. Let's examine the pattern of whole steps and half steps in the C major scale.

C Major Scale

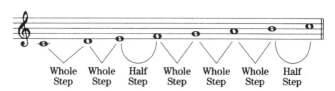

Take the time to memorize this important pattern, because it is the blueprint for all other major scales: whole step, whole step, half step, whole step, whole step, whole step, half step. Then sing or play the C major scale on the instrument of your choice.

The Sharp Keys

Once you are quite familiar with the step-by-step pattern of the C major scale, take a look at the *G major scale.* The notes of this scale are the building blocks for music in the *key of G major.* Notice that this scale requires an F♯ note in order to follow the proper step-by-step pattern for major scales.

G Major Scale

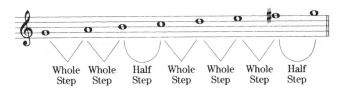

Since the F♯ note is a regular feature in the key of G major, it is represented in the key signature after the clef on every staff of the piece. This means that all notes that occur in the F position in the piece (unless otherwise marked) will be sharped—as in this excerpt from Schubert's "Unfinished Symphony."

Theme from the Unfinished Symphony

Keep in mind that the F♯ note indicated in the preceding key signature applies to all F♯ note positions in the piece, no matter how high or low. This applies to the bass clef as well.

Let's take a look at all of the major key signatures and corresponding scales that contain sharps. Although it is not necessary to include any sharp signs next to the notes of these scales, they are shown here in parentheses for your reference.

The Sharp Keys

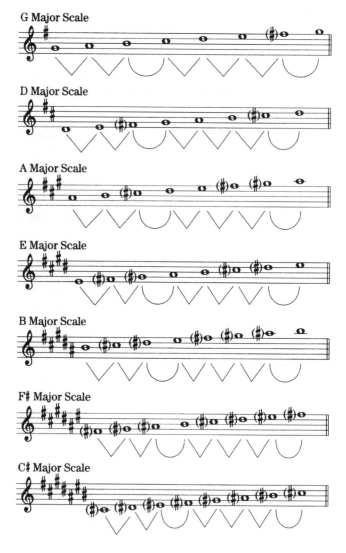

Here's a trick for identifying the major key represented by any key signature that contains sharps. Find the line or space position that is one half step higher than the position of the last sharp to the right in the key signature. This position names the major key. As you can see, this pattern is similar in both clefs.

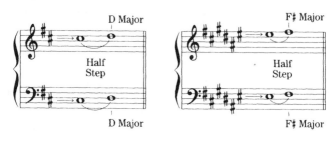

The easiest way to memorize the order of the sharps as they appear in the key signatures is to examine the pattern of sharps in the key of C♯ major, which features all seven sharps.

F   C   G   D   A   E   B

Take a look at the distance between each consecutive sharp in the key signature of C♯ major. Stepping down the staff by lines and spaces, the second sharp (C♯) is three note positions lower on the staff than the first sharp (F♯). The third sharp (G♯) is four positions higher on the staff than the second sharp (C♯)—and the fourth sharp is three steps lower than the third.

In order to avoid placing the fifth sharp of the pattern (A♯) on a leger line above the staff, this note is moved down an octave to the A♯ that occurs in the second space of the staff. The last two sharps (E♯ and B♯) return to the original pattern.

This pattern is identical in bass clef.

F   C   G   D   A   E   B

Familiarize yourself with the pattern of sharps. Practice writing the seven sharps that make up the key signature of C♯ major. Then write in the name of the major key indicated by each of these key signatures.

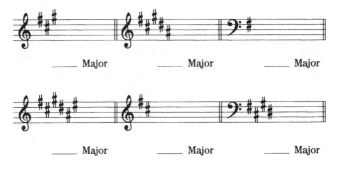

_____ Major   _____ Major   _____ Major

_____ Major   _____ Major   _____ Major

The Flat Keys

Now let's focus on the key signatures that contain flats. Here's the F major scale, which features one flat.

F Major Scale

Familiarize yourself with all of the major key signatures and corresponding scales that contain flats.

The Flat Keys

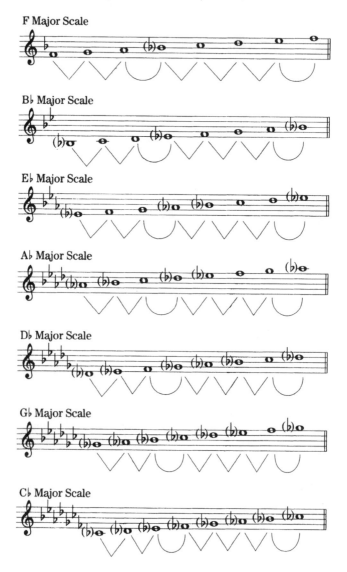

Here's a trick for identifying the major key represented by a key signature with flats. Find the second to the last flat of the key signature. Add a flat to the letter name of that note position and you've got the name of the key. (You'll need to memorize the fact that one flat indicates the key of F major.)

To understand the pattern of flats, take a look at the distance between each consecutive flat in the key signature of C♭ major. Stepping up the staff by lines and spaces, the second flat (E♭) is three note positions higher on the staff than the first flat (B♭). The third flat (A♭) is four positions lower on the staff than the second flat (E♭)—the fourth flat is three steps higher than the third, and so on.

This pattern is the same in bass clef.

Familiarize yourself with the pattern of flats. Practice writing the seven flats that make up the key signature of C♭ major. Then test your ability to identify the major keys represented by key signatures that contain flats by writing in the key names below.

Compound Time Signatures

You are already familiar with the simple time signatures, like $\frac{3}{4}$ and $\frac{4}{4}$. *Compound time signatures* obey the same rules as simple time signatures, but the rhythmic stresses they create in music are based upon beats that are always counted in multiples of three. The top number of a compound time signature is always a multiple of three to reflect this pattern of stress.

Let's look at the most common compound time signature to appear in written music, $\frac{6}{8}$. As you can see, there are six beats to the measure, with an eighth note valued at one beat.

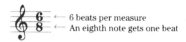

A stressed beat occurs every three eighth-note beats, providing two stresses in every measure. This pattern of stress is illustrated by boldface numbers in the first phrase of "The Irish Washerwoman."

The Irish Washerwoman

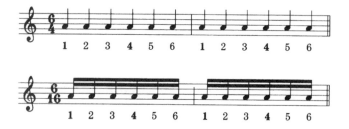

This same counting pattern occurs in music written in $\frac{6}{4}$ and $\frac{6}{16}$.

Time signatures that call for nine beats in a measure also create a stress every three beats. In $\frac{9}{8}$ time, there are three stresses in every measure.

$\frac{12}{8}$ time features twelve beats—and so four stresses— in every measure.

As with their "simple" counterparts, $\frac{3}{4}$ and $\frac{4}{4}$ time, the first stress in each measure of $\frac{9}{8}$ and $\frac{12}{8}$ time is generally the strongest. You may sometimes encounter complex time signatures—like $\frac{5}{4}$, $\frac{5}{8}$, $\frac{7}{4}$, or $\frac{7}{8}$—that call for unusual numbers of beats in each measure. These time signatures support different patterns of stress. $\frac{5}{4}$ and $\frac{7}{8}$ time are each illustrated below in typical patterns of stress.

You may find that a time signature changes in the middle of a piece to create an entirely new rhythm. This can be seen in the traditional carol "Here We Come A-Wassailing." At the beginning of the song's chorus, the timing changes from $\frac{6}{8}$ to $\frac{4}{4}$.

Here We Come A-Wassailing

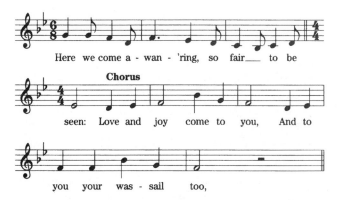

To familiarize yourself with the more commonly used compound time signatures, practice counting and playing these melody phrases.

Sweet Betsy from Pike

Barcarolle (from Tales of Hoffman*)*

Beautiful Dreamer

More About Note Values and Rhythm

By now, you are quite familiar with basic note and rest values. Let's look at some new note values and signs that express information about the rhythm of a piece of music.

Ties

Some notes are actually made up of two note values that are linked together with a *tie*. A tie indicates that a note be held for the combined length of the two tied notes. For this reason, the two notes that are tied together on the staff always have exactly the same pitch. Ties are often used to link two notes across the barline, as can be seen in the last two bars of this excerpt from "Daisy Bell."

Daisy Bell (A Bicycle Built for Two)

Sometimes tied notes are used within a bar to make the rhythm easy to count within a certain musical context.

Ties may also be used in sequence for this purpose.

If a note altered by an accidental is tied across the barline, the second note is also affected. Any subsequent notes of the same pitch will be unaffected.

Because of their similar appearance, ties are often confused with *slurs*, which are defined in the later section on accents and articulation. The way to tell them apart is to remember that ties link notes of the same pitch, while slurs always link notes of different pitches.

Extended Rests

Extended rests are used primarily in orchestral or band music since these genres often require that certain instruments rest for several bars. A numeral above the sign indicates the number of measures for which the instruments should rest. This sign indicates that the rest should last for twelve bars.

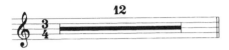

Pauses

Sometimes a composer or arranger wishes to indicate that the regular beat or tempo of a piece should hold or pause for a moment on a specific note or rest. This hold or pause is indicated with a *fermata*, as shown in the following two phrases of "For He's a Jolly Good Fellow." (The amount of time that the indicated note or rest should be held is left to the discretion of the performer.)

For He's a Jolly Good Fellow

Another kind of pause of indefinite length is indicated with two slashes above the staff (//). This marking is called a *cesura* (or *cæsura*)—and indicates that the note is held for its normal time value and then followed by an abrupt pause at the performer's discretion.

Triplets and Other Note Groupings

Composers and arrangers sometimes need to divide a basic note value into three notes of equal value. These three notes are collectively called a *triplet*, which is indicated by the numeral *3* on the beam. Each "eighth-note" in the triplet below is worth one-third of one beat. Try clapping the rhythm of "March of the Wooden Soldiers" (from *The Nutcracker*).

March of the Wooden Soldiers

Other note values may be used in a triplet. Here's an example of "quarter notes" linked in a triplet. Notice that a bracket is used when notes cannot be joined by a beam. Each of these is worth one-third of the value of a half note, or two-thirds of a beat. Play the first phrase of "Hey There, You with the Stars in Your Eyes."

Hey There, You with the Stars in Your Eyes

Triplets can also contain dotted notes and rests. Thus, in "Lilliburlero," the dotted "eighth notes" in each triplet are actually worth one-half of a beat. Each "sixteenth note" is worth one-sixth of a beat.

Lilliburlero

You may also encounter sixteenth-note or thirty-second-note triplets, as shown in this example.

Duplets do not commonly occur in popular music. They are used in music written in compound time signatures to indicate that two notes receive the value commonly afforded to three notes in that timing. The duplet in this phrase in $\frac{6}{8}$ indicates that the two "eighth-notes" are played in the time usually allotted to three eighth notes. This means that each note of the duplet is worth one and a half beats in this time signature.

Quadruplets, *quintuplets*, and *sextuplets* are also infrequent.

Intervals

The distance between two notes is called an *interval*. To understand how intervals are named, let's look at the *degrees* (or numerical names) of the notes of the C major scale.

Diatonic Intervals

Here are the intervals that correspond to the scale in C major. These are called *diatonic intervals*. Practice playing or singing these intervals until you are familiar with the name and characteristic sound of each one.

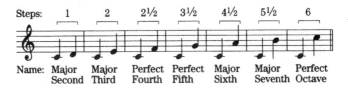

When the notes of these intervals are played simultaneously, they are called *harmonic intervals*. Listen to the notes of each interval played simultaneously on the piano or guitar.

Intervals may occur on different notes of the scale in different keys. It's easy to identify an interval by its position on the staff. For example:

 An interval of a second contains one note on a line and one note on an adjacent space.

 An interval of a third either contains two notes on adjacent lines or two notes on adjacent spaces.

 A fourth contains a note on a space and a note on a line with one line and one space in between.

 A fifth contains two notes on lines with one line skipped, or two notes on spaces with one space skipped.

 A sixth contains one note on a line and one note on a space with two lines and two spaces skipped.

A seventh contains two notes on lines with two lines skipped, or two notes on spaces with two spaces skipped.

An octave contains one note on a line and one note on a space, with three lines and three spaces skipped.

Chromatic Intervals

When a diatonic interval is made larger or smaller by an interval of a half step, a *chromatic interval* results. Let's take a look at the now familiar diatonic intervals and their corresponding lowered and raised chromatic intervals in sequence.

Chromatic Intervals (Lowered)	Diatonic Intervals	Chromatic Intervals (Raised)
Minor Second	Major Second	Augmented Second
Minor Third	Major Third	Augmented Third
Diminished Fourth	Perfect Fourth	Augmented Fourth
Diminished Fifth	Perfect Fifth	Augmented Fifth
Minor Sixth	Major Sixth	Augmented Sixth
Minor Seventh	Major Seventh	Augmented Seventh
Diminished Octave	Perfect Octave	Augmented Octave

One interval that has not been featured in the preceding charts is the *perfect unison*. The perfect unison may be diminished and augmented like any other perfect interval.

Diminished Unison   Perfect Unison   Augmented Unison

Take the time to memorize the name and appearance of each of the chromatic intervals. Play (or sing and play) each interval backward and forward until you are familiar with its sound. You'll find that certain intervals—like the augmented second and minor third—sound exactly alike. Determine which other intervals sound alike. (These intervals occur in a predictable pattern.)

When naming a chromatic interval, first determine the name of its unaltered form (second, third, fourth, and so on). Then determine the chromatic interval's name by ascertaining whether the diatonic interval has been made larger or smaller by one half-step (according to the major scale of the lower note).

Label each of these diatonic and chromatic intervals. Be sure to consider the clef and key signature of each.

It's easy to memorize intervals by associating them with familiar melodies. Here are some suggested melody phrases to use for this purpose. The indicated interval is shown in brackets. The common abbreviation for each interval is also included above the bracket.

The study and practice of intervals is central to a musician's ability to sightread written music. You may find it useful to study with a friend—and take turns playing, singing, and identifying intervals together.

Stardust / Oh Susanna!

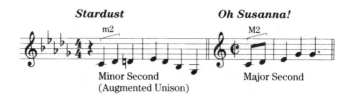

Minor Second
(Augmented Unison)

Major Second

Greensleeves / Frankie and Johnny

Minor Third
(Augmented Second)

Major Third
(Diminished Fourth)

Auld Lang Syne / Maria (from West Side Story)

Perfect Fourth
(Augmented Third)

Diminished Fifth
(Augmented Fourth)

Twinkle, Twinkle, Little Star / Let My People Go

Perfect Fifth

Minor Sixth
(Augmented Fifth)

My Bonnie / Somewhere (from West Side Story)

Major Sixth

Minor Seventh
(Augmented Sixth)

Bali Hai (from South Pacific) / Somewhere over the Rainbow

Major Seventh
(Diminished Octave)

Perfect Octave
(Augmented Seventh)

Double Sharps and Flats

Though they rarely occur, you may come across a *double sharp* or *double flat* in written music. These accidentals are seldom necessary—and keys that may require their use are generally avoided. However, double sharps or double flats are sometimes used to maintain a logical pattern of notes on the staff. A double sharp (**x**) raises the indicated note by two half-steps. If the note is already sharped in the key signature, or by a previous accidental in the same measure, the double sharp raises the pitch by one half-step only. In other words, a double sharp raises any note two half-steps from its natural position. Thus, F**x** is another name for the G note.

An F**x** note is used in the following example to preserve the visual pattern of ascending thirds in the key of E major.

If a G note were used instead of F**x** in this passage, the pattern of thirds would be violated, and thus more difficult to read.

Sometimes a *natural sharp sign* is used to return a double sharp note to a sharped note in the same measure. However, a sharp sign alone is sufficient.

You may also sometimes see a double natural employed to cancel a double sharp completely in the same measure. However, a single natural sign is sufficient.

A double flat sign lowers the indicated note by two half steps. Here, B♭♭ is used to preserve the pattern of descending thirds in the key of E-flat major.

Minor Keys and Scales

Sometimes a composer or arranger chooses to write in a particular key to lend a special tonal color, or *tonality*, to a piece. Many of the musical excerpts you have studied so far have been written in a major key, and therefore have major tonalities. Composers often choose a *minor key* to lend an introspective or sad quality to a piece.

There are three forms of the minor scale: the *natural minor*, the *melodic minor*, and the *harmonic minor*. Let's compare the familiar C major scale with the minor forms. Since all C minor scales use the same starting note as the C major scale, they are called the *tonic minor* of this major key. For this same reason, C major and C minor are also sometimes called *parallel keys*. Notice that the third, sixth, and seventh notes of the natural minor scale are lowered by one half-step. The melodic minor features a lowered third on the way up the scale, and a lowered third, sixth, and seventh on the way down. The third and sixth of the harmonic minor scale are lowered by a half-step, whether ascending or descending.

C Major Scale

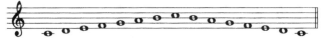

C Natural Minor Scale

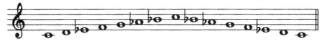

C Melodic Minor Scale

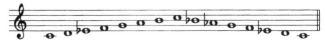

C Harmonic Minor Scale

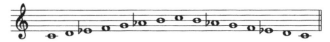

In order to avoid the routine writing of the accidentals necessary to create these minor forms, music written in the key of C minor features a key signature with three flats (like the key of E-flat major). This brings the need for accidentals to a minimum. In this key signature, an accidental is required only on the sixth and seventh degrees of the ascending C melodic minor scale—and on the seventh degree of the C harmonic minor scale.

C Melodic Minor Scale

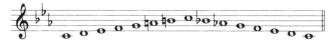

C Harmonic Minor Scale

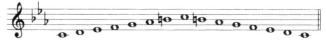

Because the key of C minor uses the same key signature as E-flat major, it is known as the *relative minor* of this major key. Correspondingly, the key of E-flat major is known as the *relative major* of C minor. Presented below are all the harmonic and melodic scale forms in every minor key. The name of each relative major key is shown in parentheses. Notice that the relative major key is always three half-steps (a minor third) up from the note named by the corresponding minor key.

Sharp Keys

Key of A Minor (Relative Minor of C Major)

A Melodic Minor Scale

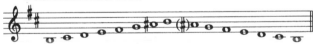

A Harmonic Minor Scale

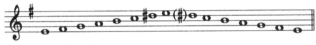

Key of E Minor (Relative Minor of G Major)

E Melodic Minor Scale

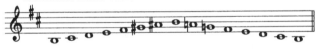

E Harmonic Minor Scale

Key of B Minor (Relative Minor of D Major)

B Melodic Minor Scale

B Harmonic Minor Scale

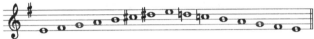

Key of F# Minor (Relative Minor of A Major)

F# Melodic Minor Scale

F# Harmonic Minor Scale

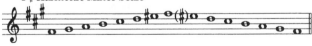

Key of C# Minor (Relative Minor of E Major)

C# Melodic Minor Scale

C# Harmonic Minor Scale

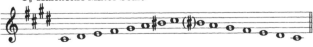

Key of G♯ Minor (Relative Minor of B Major)

G♯ Melodic Minor Scale

G♯ Harmonic Minor Scale

Key of D♯ Minor (Relative Minor of F♯ Major)

D♯ Melodic Minor Scale

D♯ Harmonic Minor Scale

Key of A♯ Minor (Relative Minor of C♯ Major)

A♯ Melodic Minor Scale

A♯ Harmonic Minor Scale

Flat Keys

Key of D Minor (Relative Minor of F Major)

D Melodic Minor Scale

D Harmonic Minor Scale

Key of G Minor (Relative Minor of B♭ Major)

G Melodic Minor Scale

G Harmonic Minor Scale

Key of C Minor (Relative Minor of E♭ Major)

C Melodic Minor Scale

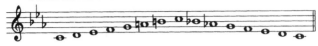

C Harmonic Minor Scale

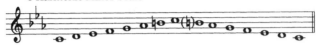

Key of F Minor (Relative Minor of A♭ Major)

F Melodic Minor Scale

F Harmonic Minor Scale

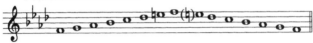

Key of B♭ Minor (Relative Minor of D♭ Major)

B♭ Melodic Minor Scale

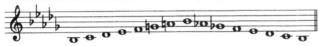

B♭ Harmonic Minor Scale

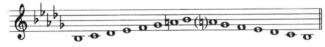

Key of E♭ Minor (Relative Minor of G♭ Major)

E♭ Melodic Minor Scale

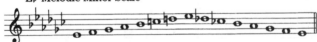

E♭ Harmonic Minor Scale

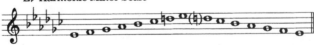

Key of A♭ Minor (Relative Minor of C♭ Major)

A♭ Melodic Minor Scale

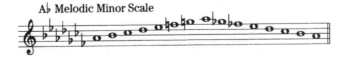

A♭ Harmonic Minor Scale

Structure

In basic terms, a musical composition should have a clear beginning that leads to the body of the piece (often called the *development section*) and an effective ending.

Many songs feature an *introduction* or *verse* section as an opener—leading to the *chorus* or main section of the piece. Classical compositions use various conventions for arranging the individual sections of a work.

Let's look at the different markings that guide the musician through the sections of a musical composition. The thumbnail examples used in this section illustrate the functions of these markings. In a full-sized musical composition, several pages of music may actually occur between symbols—so it's a good idea to review their placement and meaning before you begin to play or sing.

Repeat Sign

Most styles of music call for their individual sections to be repeated at times. In fact, this kind of repetition is often important to the structure of a musical composition. Two dots before a double bar form a *repeat sign*.

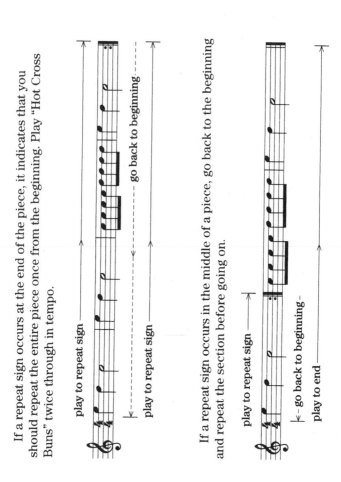

Inverted Repeat Sign

If a reverse repeat sign occurs earlier in the piece, you should only repeat from that point onward. Here the inverted repeat sign means that you should skip the first measure when you repeat the piece.

play to repeat sign

go back to inverted repeat sign

play to repeat sign

Da Capo

D.C. is an abbreviation of the Italian phrase *Da Capo*, meaning "from the head." This marking means the same thing as a single repeat sign—repeat the piece from its beginning.

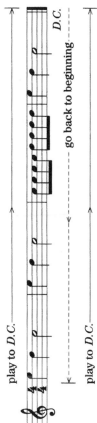

play to D.C.

go back to beginning

play to D.C.

D.C.

Dal Segno

D.S. stands for the Italian phrase *Dal Segno* (pronounced "dahl senyo"), meaning "from the sign." D.S. means to go back to the dal segno sign (𝄋) and repeat the section.

play to D.S.

go back to 𝄋

play to D.S.

D.S.

Alternate Endings

A bracket and numeral is used to mark alternate endings for a section. Here you should skip the *first ending* on the repeat and go on to the *second ending*.

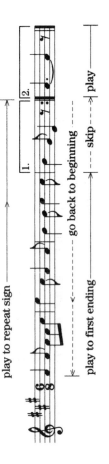

play to repeat sign

1.

2.

go back to beginning

play to first ending — skip — play

D.C. al Coda

D.C. al Coda tells you to repeat the piece until you reach the coda sign (✛)—then skip to the next coda sign, and play the *coda*, a short ending section (literally "tail").

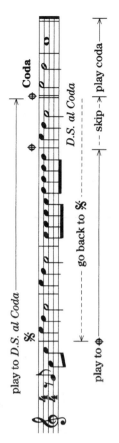

D.S. al Coda

D.S. al Coda means to repeat from the dal segno sign. Once you reach the coda sign, skip to the next coda sign, and play the coda section. *D.C. al Coda* and *D.S. al Coda* are also written *D.C. al* ✛ and *D.S. al* ✛.

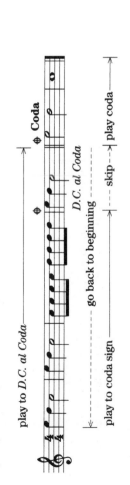

D.C. al Fine

Fine (pronounced "feenay") is the Italian word for "end." *D.C. al Fine* tells you to go back to the beginning of the piece and repeat until you come to the marking *Fine*.

D.S. al Fine

D.S. al Fine means to go back to the dal segno sign and repeat until the point marked *Fine*.

Accents and Articulations

Different accents and articulations are used to create distinctive phrases and textures in a piece.

Staccato

If a dot appears above or below a note, that note should be played or sung with a short and crisp action called *staccato.* Staccato notes with upward stems feature the dot beneath the notehead. Notes with downward stems feature the dot above the notehead. In order to create a short, sharp sound, a staccato note receives less than half its indicated value. For example, each of these quarter notes is approximately equivalent to a sixteenth note, as shown.

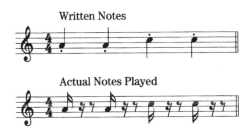

A triangle above or below a note also indicates that it should be treated as a staccato, though this marking generally calls for somewhat more stress.

Accents

Notes marked with any of these *accent signs* should be played or sung with a strong accent and held for their full note value.

The symbols *sf, sz,* and *sfz* (short for *sforzando*), as well as *rf* (short for *rinforzando*), indicate that a very strong accent be applied to the designated note.

Slur

A curved line connecting two or more notes calls for
them to be played smoothly. The *slur* should not be
confused with the *tie*, which calls for two notes of the
same pitch to be played as one note value.

Sometimes a slur is used with staccato markings to
indicate that the notes be played halfway between
staccato and legato—that is, they are still detached, yet
somewhat smooth.

Phrase Mark

A *phrase mark* is a curved line used by composers and
arrangers to indicate the natural punctuation of a musical
piece. Phrase marks are usually used to highlight longer
passages than slurs, as shown in the first two phrases of
"Twinkle, Twinkle, Little Star." Notice that a tie also
appears in the last measures of this example.

Twinkle, Twinkle, Little Star

When used in a song, phrase marks often correspond
with the natural punctuation of its lyrics. This type of
agreement of phrasing between melody and lyrics helps
make a song memorable and structurally sound.

Ornaments

Ornaments are musical decorations that provide points of interest in a piece.

Grace Notes

The *grace note* is a small note that adjoins a full-sized note. It is usually depicted as a small eighth note with a slash through its flag and stem. The grace note you will encounter most often in written music is the *unaccented grace note*. This note should be played as quickly as possible just before the natural beat of the note that follows. Here is the grace note, both as it is notated and as it is actually played.

A grace note that features an accent sign is called an *accented grace note* or *appoggiatura*. This note should be played as quickly as possible on the natural beat of the note that follows. Thus, the value of the grace note is deducted from that of the full-sized note, as shown.

Grace notes may also occur in groups. These are usually unaccented grace notes and their time value is deducted from that of the previous beat. A group of two or three grace notes usually features two beams, like sixteenth notes. Groups of four or more grace notes feature three beams, like thirty-second notes. Multiple grace notes should be played quite quickly, according to the skill and taste of the performer.

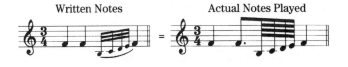

Trills

A *trill* is an ornament that consists of the rapid alternation of a note with the note above it. A trill lasts for the full length of the indicated note. Here is a quarter note with a trill, and an illustration of how the trill is actually played.

Longer trills usually include a wavy line after the trill symbol.

Tremolo

A *tremolo* is indicated by two half notes joined together with a beam. This means that these two pitches should each be played twice in an alternating pattern of eighth notes.

When half notes are joined with a double beam, the two notes are played four times each in an alternating pattern of sixteenth notes. A triple beam indicates that you play eight alternating thirty-second notes—which, in effect, means to play the alternating pattern as quickly as possible. Tremolos may be applied to other note values.

In music for stringed instruments, the term tremolo is used to indicate the rapid repetition of the same note. This figure is indicated with two or three slash marks through the notes stem, as shown.

Turns

A turn symbol (∾ or ∿) placed over a note indicates that a certain pattern of notes should be played or sung, as shown.

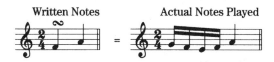

If a turn symbol appears after a note, the pattern begins on the second half of the beat.

An inverted turn is marked with an inverted turn symbol (∾), indicating that the turn begin on the note below the written note. (The inverted turn may also be indicated with these symbols ⌘ and ✚.)

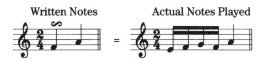

If the inverted turn symbol is placed after a note, the pattern begins on the second half of the beat.

Mordents

The *mordent* symbol calls for the quick alternation of the written note with the note above it, as shown.

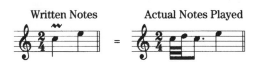

The *lower mordent* calls for the alternation of the written note with the note below it. This ornament appears more commonly than the mordent, which is sometimes called the *upper mordent*.

Tempo

The overall speed of a piece of music is called its *tempo*. Composers and arrangers often indicate approximately how fast a piece should be performed by using an Italian or English term on top of the staff at the beginning of a piece or section. Here are some common Italian tempo markings.

Lento (or **Largo**) = Very slow
Adagio = Slow
Andante = Walking pace
Moderato = Medium
Allegretto = Medium fast
Allegro = Fast
Presto = Very fast
Prestissimo = As fast as possible

Certain terms call for a changing tempo. The term *rallentando* indicates that the tempo should slow down. *Ritardando* (often abbreviated as *ritard.* or *rit.*) has the same meaning. *Accelerando* calls for a quickening of the tempo. The term *a tempo* tells the musician to return to the normal speed of the piece. *Rubato* indicates that the tempo should speed up and slow down according to taste.

The *metronome* is a device that taps out beats at regular intervals. The metronome's speed may be adjusted, and so it is useful to musicians for setting regular and precise tempos during practice. A *metronome marking* at the beginning of a piece or section indicates the number of beats per minute. This marking indicates sixty quarter notes per minute (so each quarter note lasts one second). This is a moderately slow tempo.

Compositions with time signatures that call for a half note, dotted quarter, or eighth note to equal one beat may include metronome markings with these notes. Each of the metronome markings that follow represent a moderate tempo (moderato).

Here are some other examples of metronome markings. From left to right they indicate these tempos: adagio, moderato, allegro, and presto.

Expression

Certain Italian and English words are used to indicate that a piece or section be played with a particular expressive quality.

Agitato = Agitated
Animato = Animated
Appassionato = With passion
Bravura = Boldly
Brillante = Brilliantly
Cantabile = As if sung
Con anima = With feeling
Con moto = With movement
Con spirito = With spirit
Dolce = Sweetly
Doloroso = Sorrowfully

Energico = Energetically
Espressivo = Expressively
Facile = Easily
Grave = Slow and solemn
Legato = Smoothly
Maestoso = Majestically
Mesto = Sadly
Scherzando = Playfully
Semplice = Simply
Sostenuto = Sustained
Vivace = Lively

Dynamics

Terms or symbols that indicate volume are called *dynamic markings*. Italian or English terms may be used at the beginning of a piece to indicate overall volume. Symbols are often used to abbreviate these words, especially when volume changes occur during the piece. Take the time to memorize these common dynamic symbols and their meanings.

ppp = Pianississimo = As soft as possible
pp = Pianissimo = Very soft
p = Piano = Soft
mp = Mezzo piano = Moderately soft
mf = Mezzo forte = Moderately loud
f = Forte = Loud
ff = Fortissimo = Very loud
fff = Fortississimo = As loud as possible

An increase in volume is indicated by the term *crescendo* (or *cresc.*). The terms *decrescendo* and *diminuendo* (or *dim.*) indicate a decrease in volume. Volume changes for specific notes are indicated with a crescendo or diminuendo symbol. A crescendo, followed by a decrescendo is indicated in the last four bars of "For He's a Jolly Good Fellow." (The relative length of these symbols indicates the notes included in the volume change.)

For He's a Jolly Good Fellow

READING TABLATURE

Tablature is a well-known system of notation designed specially for guitarists. The tablature staff is composed of six lines. Each line represents a string of the guitar, with string **1** being the highest, and string **6**, the lowest.

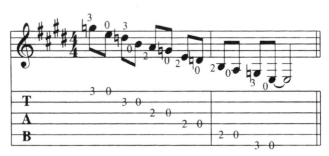

Fret numbers placed on the lines of guitar tablature tell you which fret to play on a given string. (Fret **1** is the fret nearest to the tuning pegs and **0** indicates an unfretted or *open string*.) When fingering numbers are included, they appear with the notes on the staff: 1=index finger, 2=middle finger, 3=ring finger, and 4=pinky.

The first-position *E pentatonic blues scale* is shown below in music notation and guitar tablature. Play this descending scale several times in tempo. Use your middle finger (2) for notes on the second fret and your ring finger (3) for notes on the third fret, as indicated.

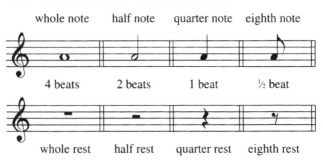

While guitar tablature shows you which frets and strings to play, you must get the rhythm from the notes on the music staff. Here are four standard note values and rests—and their relative duration in beats.

whole note	half note	quarter note	eighth note
4 beats	2 beats	1 beat	½ beat
whole rest	half rest	quarter rest	eighth rest

Now play the same descending E pentatonic blues scale in a new rhythmic pattern as you count aloud.

Hammerons, Pulloffs, Slides, and Bends

Hammeron. A slur connecting two ascending notes indicates a hammeron. Play the open first string. While the note is sounding, bring the ring finger (3) of your left hand down at the third fret to play the second note.

Pulloff. A slur connecting two descending notes indicates a pulloff. Fret the first string with your ring finger (3) at the third fret—then play the first note. While the note is still ringing, pluck the string with your left-hand third finger to sound the open-string note.

Slide. A slur and a diagonal line between two notes indicates a slide. Fret the third string with your middle finger (2) at the second fret. Then play the note and quickly slide this finger up the string to the fourth fret.

Bend. A slur (with the letter **B**) connecting two notes indicates a bend. Fret the second string with your ring finger (3) at the fifth fret—and play the first note. While the note is sounding, push the string upward to bend the pitch up to the higher note (shown in parentheses).

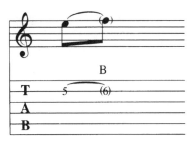

Other Tablature Symbols

Some publications use different symbols to notate bends. These are shown below, along with a few other symbols indicating other common playing techniques.

SEMI-TONE BEND: Strike the note and bend up a semi-tone (1/2 step).

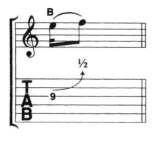

WHOLE-TONE BEND: Strike the note and bend up a whole-tone (whole step).

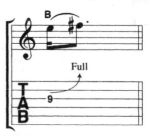

BEND & RELEASE: Strike the note and bend up as indicated, then release back to the original note.

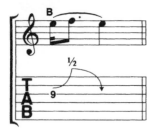

BEND & RESTRIKE: Strike the note and bend as indicated then restrike the string where the symbol occurs.

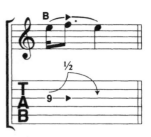

NATURAL HARMONIC: Strike the note while the fret-hand lightly touches the string directly over the fret indicated.

PICK SCRAPE: The edge of the pick is rubbed down (or up) the string, producing a scratchy sound.

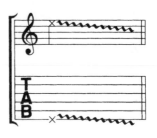

NOTE: The speed of any bend is indicated by the music notation and tempo.

GRACE NOTE BEND: Strike the note and bend as indicated. Play the first note as quickly as possible.

QUARTER-TONE BEND: Strike the note and bend up a 1/4 step.

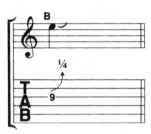

PRE-BEND: Bend the note as indicated, then strike it.

PRE-BEND & RELEASE: Bend the note as indicated. Strike it and release the note back to the original pitch.

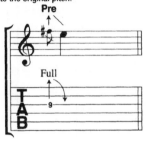

PALM MUTING: The note is muted by the pick hand lightly touching the string(s) just before the bridge.

MUFFLED STRINGS: A percussive sound is produced by laying the fret hand across the string(s) without depressing, and striking them with the pick hand.

Table of Notes

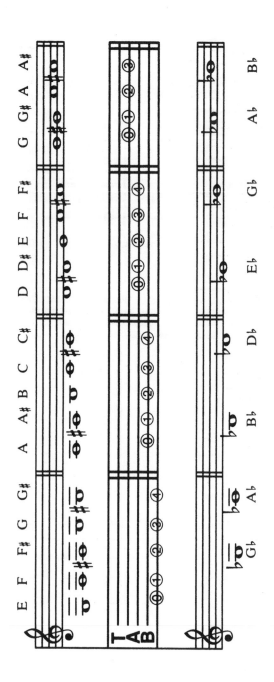

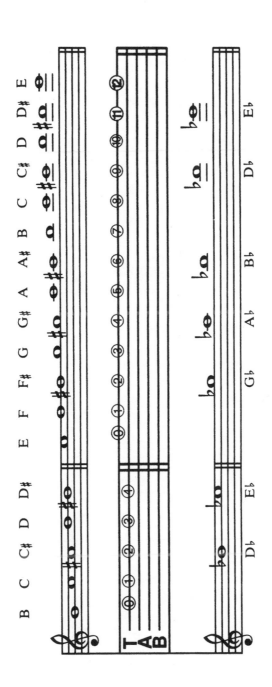

CHORD CHART

A *chord chart* is an arrangement of a song that contains chord symbols only. Take a look at the chord chart for the rock/blues song entitled "Crossroad Blues." A basic chord chart like this one need only show the general outline of the harmony: the name and duration of each chord. Here, four slash marks in each measure represent the four quarter-note beats per measure in $\frac{4}{4}$ time.

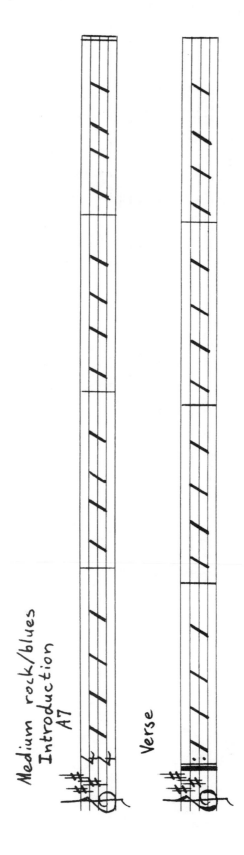

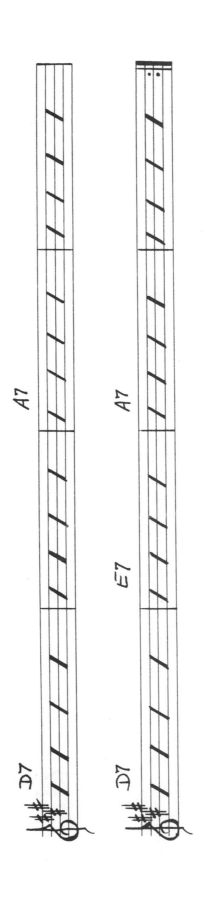

LEAD SHEET

A *lead sheet* is a written version of a song that contains the melody, chord symbols, and lyrics. Here's "Crossroad Blues" in lead sheet form. You should create a lead sheet like this for every song you write. In this sample lead sheet, the important elements are labeled with the circled letters A through K. You'll find a complete legend of definitions on the page that follows.

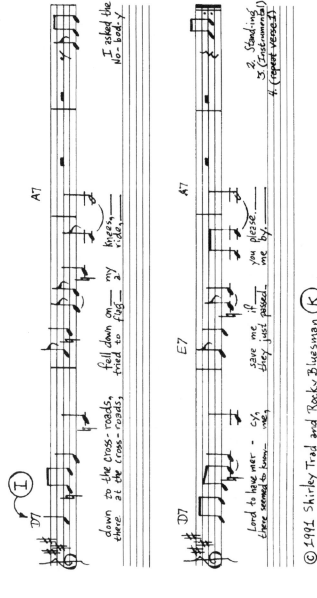

© 1991 Shirley Trad and Rocky Bluesman Ⓚ

Key to Lead Sheet

A) Title. The title appears at the top and center of the first page of the lead sheet. When creating your own lead sheet, use initial capitals on all title words with four letters or more. Always use initial capitals on the first and last word of a title. Don't capitalize articles ("a," "an," and "the"), conjunctions ("and" and "but"), or prepositions ("on," "in," "out," and so on). Capitalize prepositions that are part of a verbal phrase (as in "Roll Out the Barrel"). Avoid subtitles or alternate titles that detract from your phrase of choice.

B) Lyricist/Composer. Use initial capitals to credit the lyricist and composer. If the words and music are created by one person, write "Words and music by [name]" in this position.

C) Tempo/Feel. Indicate the tempo or feel of a song in this position. Here, a simple instruction like "Medium rock" or "Slow shuffle" is often most useful. Only the first word of the tempo indication should be capitalized.

D) Treble Clef. Except in special cases, a lead sheet should be notated in the treble clef. This clef should appear at the beginning of every staff line.

D) Key Signature. The sharps and flats indicating the key appear at the beginning of every staff of the lead sheet.

E) Time Signature. The time signature is written after the key signature at the beginning of the first staff only.

F) Riff Figure. Some of the songs you write may feature an important instrumental riff as an integral part of the song structure. In this example, the riff figure forms the introduction. Don't feel the need to add a riff figure to your lead sheet unless it really needs one.

G) Melody. The complete melody of the song should be clearly notated on the staff. There's no need to write special instructions to the vocalist or notate melody nuances that can be worked out later. The melody should be notated in its simplest form.

H) Lyric. Each syllable of the lyric should correspond with one or more melody notes. Hyphens divide words into syllables. If one syllable lasts for more than one note, the hyphen is centered under the corresponding melody notes. If a word (or the last syllable of a word) is held for two melody notes, it is followed by a horizontal underline. One or two extra verses may be included beneath the first verse (in which case, the verses should be numbered "1," "2," "3," and so on). Some songs feature more than one or two extra verses. These should appear at the bottom of the lead sheet in block text (and numbered "2," "3," "4," and so on).

I) Chord Symbols. The lead sheet includes chord letter names outlining the harmonic structure of a song. Try not to use unnecessarily complex chords here. Just reduce the harmony to its simple important movements.

J) Section Labels. It's helpful to include song section labels—like Introduction, Verse, Chorus, and Tag—to clarify the overall structure of the song.

K) Copyright Notice. Your song is protected by copyright law as soon as it is written. It's a good idea to include a copyright notice at the bottom of your lead sheet with the year and the name of the song's rightful owner.

3

Guitar Scale Dictionary

Scales can do wonders for your playing if you practice them regularly—and if you understand how the different types of scales are constructed. The more scales you are familiar with, the more choices you'll have when building riffs for an arrangement or improvised solo.

The book provides a guide to scale theory and a comprehensive listing of scales in guitar tablature. Here you will find standard, altered, embellished, and open-string scales—as well as some truly exotic scales from different cultures.

Scale Basics

Simply defined, a scale is a series of tones organized in a pattern of intervals. The smallest interval is the *half step,* which corresponds to the difference in pitch between two notes one fret apart on the same string.

A distance of two half steps is a whole step.

Most scales are defined by their pattern of whole and half steps. If you know a scale pattern, you can construct that scale beginning on any note. Take a look at the pattern of intervals in the major scale.

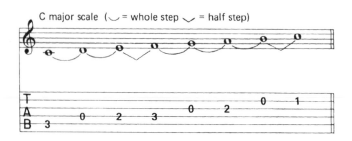

The formula of whole-whole-half-whole-whole-whole-half is the same for any major scale.

Major Scales

If you look at the C major scale shown in two halves, you can see that each half has the same formula of whole and half steps—that is, whole-whole-half. These two halves are separated by one whole-step. This means that the second half of the C major scale can start off a new major scale. Since this new scale begins on the G note, it is said to have a *tonal center* of G, and identified as the *G major scale*.

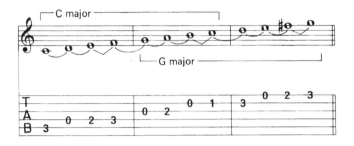

To keep the pattern of whole and half steps found in all major scales, the seventh degree of the G major scale must be sharped. Since the formula must be consistent, the G major scale will always contain an F♯, the *key signature* of the key of G major is written as shown.

Let's now take the second half of the G scale and use it as the first half of a new major scale. Notice that we have dropped the G major scale down an octave to put the new scale in a range that is easy to play.

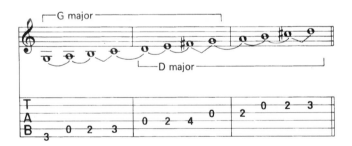

In the same way that the F♯ was added to the G scale, a C♯ must be added to the D scale to make it agree with the major scale formula. This means that the key signature of D major contains two sharps, F and C.

Continuing this process of taking the second half of a major scale to be the first half of the next will produce twelve distinct major scales each with its own distinct key signature. Notice that it is necessary to use flats rather than sharps to produce the scales in the second column of the following chart.

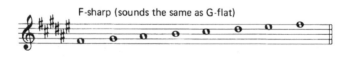

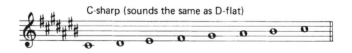

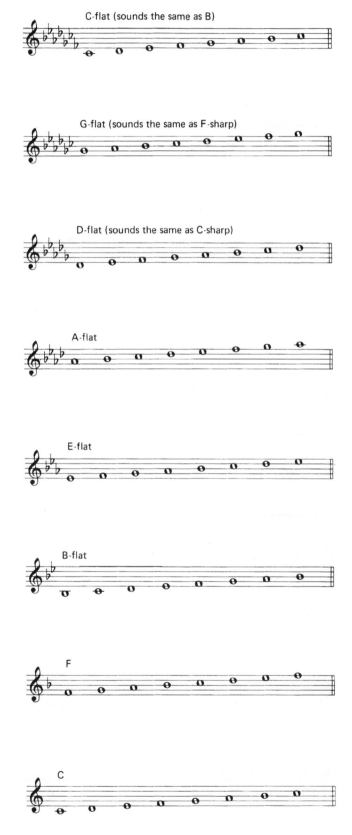

In-Position Major Scale Patterns

These scales are remarkably versatile tools. They give you seven starting points for basic major scales within one position on the neck. They are all moveable forms (containing no open strings), and each one covers a little over two octaves.

If you really have a command of these forms, you will find that you can play any major (or modal) scale within one fret of any position you may be in.

Note that although each of these stays within one four-fret position, some of them contain stretches up with the fourth finger or down with the first finger. These stretches are indicated by the letter *s*.

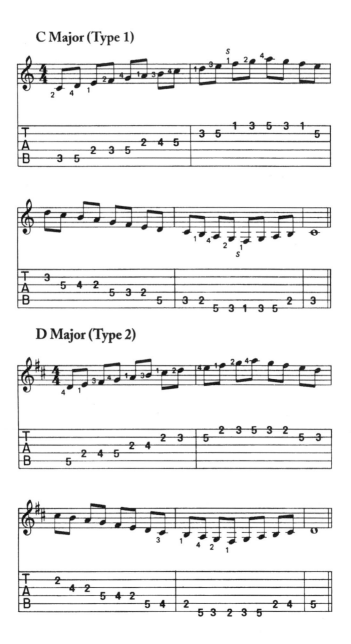

C Major (Type 1)

D Major (Type 2)

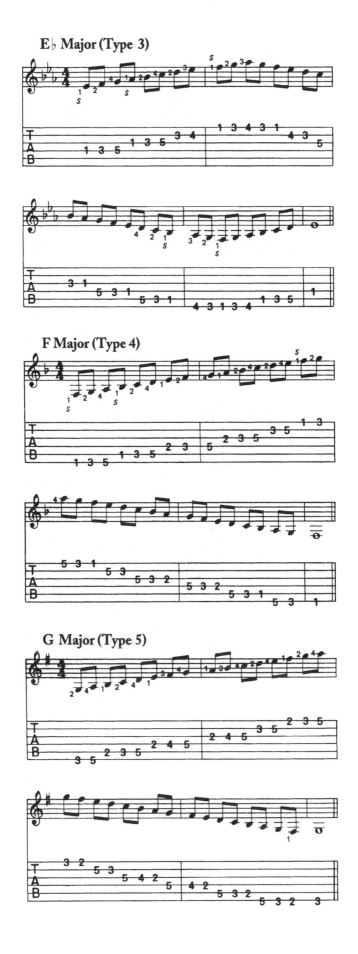

A Major (Type 6)

B♭ Major (Type 7)

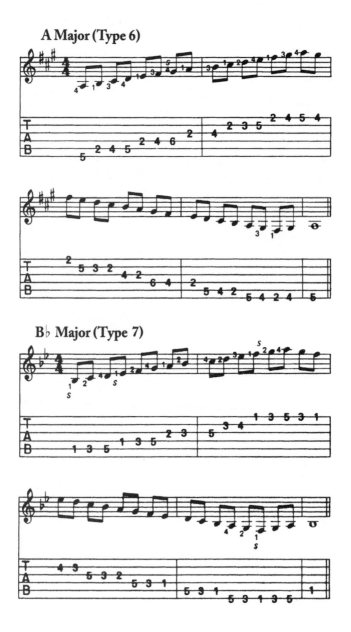

Here's an idea for practicing these scales that will really get them under your fingers: Play each scale form starting from the same root. For example, if you were to start from G-flat, the C scale form would be moved to eighth position, the D scale form to sixth position, the E-flat to fifth position, and so on. This would give you the G-flat scale in all seven positions.

Modulating Major Scales

The *circle of fifths* provides a useful pattern for practicing an extended scale pattern that *modulates* through all twelve keys. You can use this pattern (and variations on it) to practice many types of advanced scales using the full range of the fretboard. The circle of fifths begins with the key of C major, progresses clockwise through the twelve major keys, then returns to the key of C. Note that certain keys share a position on the circle of fifths (B/C♭, F♯/G♭, and C♯/D♭). The keys within each pair are called *enharmonic equivalents*. Thus B major is the enharmonic equivalent of C♭ major, and vice versa. Although these two scales sound exactly alike, they are notated as different keys (depending on the harmonic context of a particular piece of music). To avoid repetition, the most commonly used scale of each enharmonic pair is presented in the scale exercises that follow.

Circle of Fifths

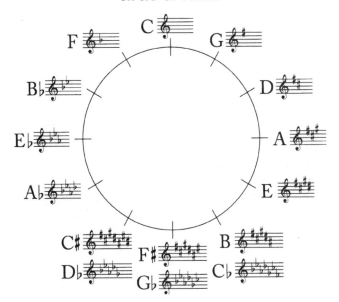

Modulating Major Scale Patterns

The circle of fifths provides the blueprint for this scale pattern, which begins in the key of C and ends in the key of F.

C Major (Type 1)

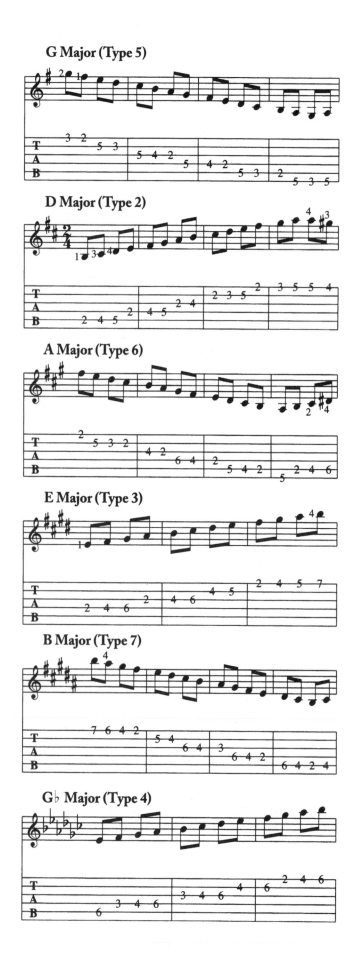

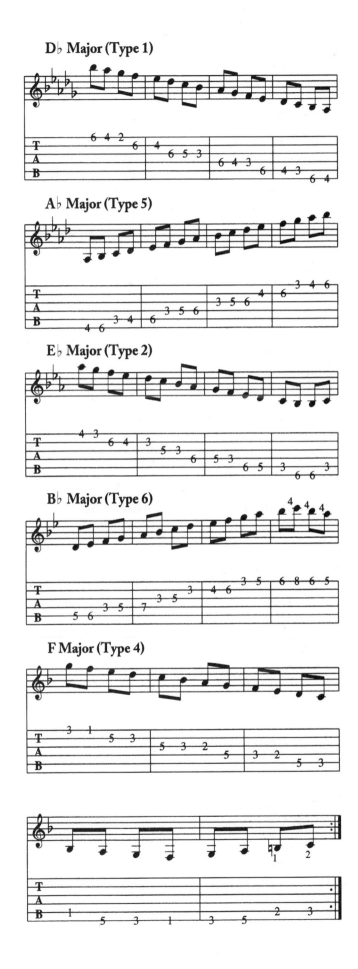

Db Major (Type 1)

Ab Major (Type 5)

Eb Major (Type 2)

Bb Major (Type 6)

F Major (Type 4)

MINOR SCALES

There are three basic types of minor scale: natural, harmonic, and melodic. These scales commonly occur in all genres of music, past and present.

Natural Minor Scale

Every one of the major scales has a corresponding *relative minor* scale that shares the same key signature. These are also called *natural minor* scales because they occur naturally, without deviating from their key signatures.

You can find the starting note of a major scale's relative minor scale by going up to the sixth degree of that scale.

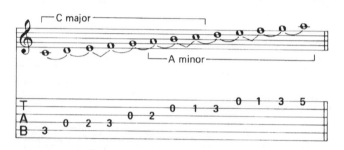

Any of the in-position major scale forms may be transformed into a natural minor scale by simply starting on the sixth degree. Thus C major becomes A minor, D major becomes B minor, and so forth, as shown in the chart below.

Major and Relative Minor Keys

Major Key	Relative Minor
C Major (no sharps or flats)	A Minor
G Major (one sharp: F♯)	E Minor
D Major (two sharps: F♯, C♯)	B Minor
A Major (three sharps: F♯, C♯, G♯)	F-sharp Minor
E Major (four sharps: F♯, C♯, G♯, D♯)	C-sharp Minor
B Major (five sharps: F♯, C♯, G♯, D♯, A♯)	G-sharp Minor
F-sharp Major (six sharps: F♯, C♯, G♯, D♯, A♯, E♯)	D-sharp Minor
C-sharp Major (seven sharps: F♯, C♯, G♯, D♯, A♯, E♯, B♯)	A-sharp Minor
F Major (one flat: B♭)	D Minor
B-flat Major (two flats: B♭, E♭)	G Minor
E-flat Major (three flats: B♭, E♭, A♭)	C Minor
A-flat Major (four flats: B♭, E♭, A♭, D♭)	F Minor
D-flat Major (five flats: B♭, E♭, A♭, D♭, G♭)	B-flat Minor
G-flat Major (six flats: B♭, E♭, A♭, D♭, G♭, C♭)	E-flat Minor
C-flat Major (seven flats: B♭, E♭, A♭, D♭, G♭, C♭, F♭)	A-flat Minor

Harmonic Minor Scale

The *harmonic minor* scale is formed by raising the seventh degree of the natural minor. Notice that the formula for a harmonic minor scale includes one interval that is neither a whole step nor a half step. The *minor third*, abbreviated *m3*, is equal to three half-steps.

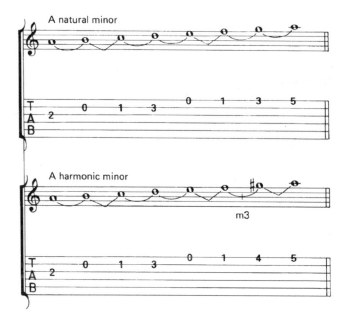

Harmonic Minor Scale Patterns

The seven harmonic minor scale patterns below are in-position scales that can be moved anywhere on the neck.

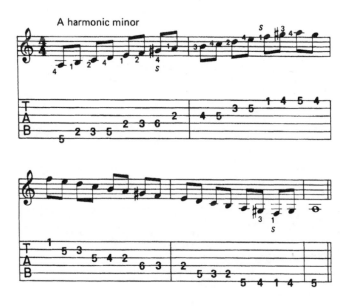

Melodic Minor Scale

The *melodic minor* scale is produced by raising the sixth and
seventh degrees of the natural minor scale.

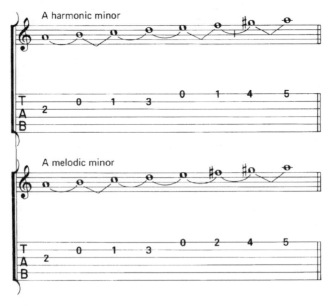

Traditionally, the melodic minor scale form follows the formula of the natural minor when descending. (If you use the
same pattern descending as ascending, this scale is called the
jazz melodic minor.)

Melodic Minor Scale Patterns

The seven melodic minor scale patterns below are in-position
scales that can be moved anywhere on the neck.

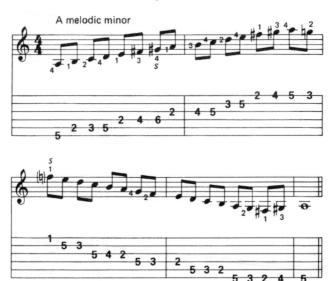

MODES

Modes are produced by displacing the starting point of a scale without changing its interval formula. This has the effect of turning out a scale with a new arrangement of whole and half steps. Most often, when musicians talk about modes they are referring to the seven modes of the major scale, although modes may be generated from any scale at all.

The modes are known by their Greek names (which were given to them by some rather creative Medieval theoreticians and have very little to do with Greece or Greek music).

The Dorian Mode

Starting on the second degree of a major scale yields a *Dorian* scale. This scale is very useful in jazz and jazz/rock—in which it's used for soloing over minor seventh chords—and sounds like the natural minor with a raised sixth.

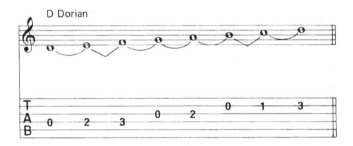

The Phrygian Mode

Playing a C major from E to E gives us an E *Phrygian* scale. This mode is reminiscent of flamenco music and sounds like the natural minor with a flatted second.

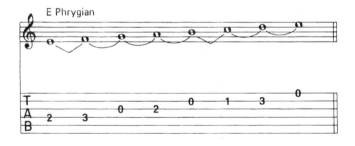

The Lydian Mode

The mode starting on the fourth degree of the major scale is known as a *Lydian* scale. This one has a major sound but differs from a straight major scale in its sharped fourth. In jazz, Lydian mode scales are generally used for soloing over major seventh chords other than the I chord.

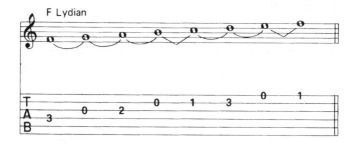

The Mixolydian Mode

Starting on the fifth degree of a major scale produces another major-sounding scale, the *Mixolydian,* with a flatted seventh. You will hear this one a lot in folk and rock music.

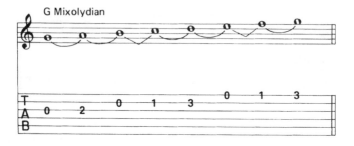

The Aeolian Mode

Remember that starting on the sixth degree of a major scale produces its relative minor. In the terminology of the modes, major is called *Ionian* and natural minor, *Aeolian.*

The Locrian Mode

The seventh mode, *Locrian,* was avoided for centuries due to its truly weird flavor. Because the scale outlines a diminished chord, melodies written in the Locrian mode never seem to quite come to rest. Inasmuch as this is sometimes a desirable quality in modern music, this mode has come into its own during the twentieth century. Also, the Locrian is useful in jazz soloing where it is commonly played over minor seventh flat-five (half-diminished) chords.

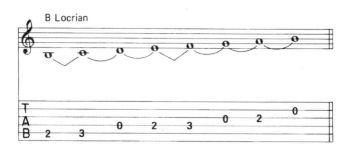

Parallel Modes

The seven modal scales that share the same starting note (or *tonic*) are called *parallel modal scales*. For example, A Dorian is a parallel modal scale of A Phrygian. The seven parallel modes of any given tonic are derived from seven different major scales. Take a look at the major scales used to produce the seven parallel modal scales that begin on an A note.

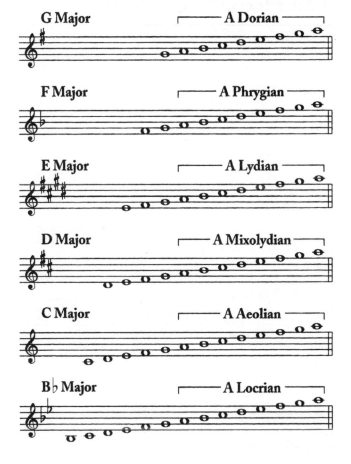

The scale pattern that follows features the seven parallel modes that begin on an A note. Notice that the key signature changes with each new mode.

Parallel Modal Scale Patterns

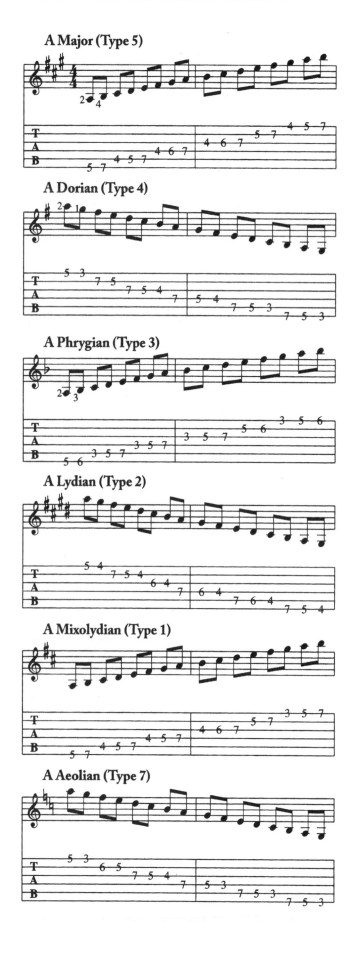

A Locrian (Type 6)

A Major (Type 5)

Once you are familiar with this scale pattern, play it again using a different tonic note to explore seven parallel modes in a new key. (Just refer to the following section, "Transposing Modal Scales," to determine the key signature, position, and fingering type to use for any given modal scale.)

For example, here's how you would begin a one-octave version of the same pattern for the seven parallel modes that begin on an E note.

E Major (Type 3)   **E Dorian (Type 2)**

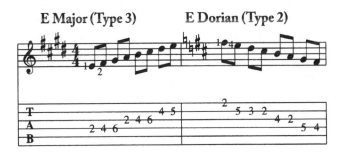

E Phrygian (Type 1)   **E Lydian (Type 7)**

etc.

Transposing Modal Scales

The chart below allows you to find the key signature for any mode. So, to play a C Dorian scale, begin on a C note, but use the key signature of B♭ (two flats). Or, to play a B♯ Locrian scale, start on B♯, but use the key signature of C♯. Enharmonic equivalents are linked by brackets at the left. Note that some of these key signatures are used for fewer than six modal scales.

Key Signatures for Modes
(Shows the major key signature for each mode in every key)

	Dorian	Phrygian	Lydian	Mixolydian	Aeolian	Locrian
[B♯	—	—	—	—	—	C♯
[C	B♭	A♭	G	F	E♭	D♭
[C♯	B	A	—	F♯	E	D
[D♭	C♭	—	A♭	G♭	—	—
D	C	B♭	A	G	F	E♭
[D♯	C♯	B	—	—	F♯	E
[E♭	D♭	C♭	B♭	A♭	G♭	—
[E	D	C	B	A	G	F
[F♭	—	—	C♭	—	—	—
[E♯	—	C♯	—	—	—	F♯
[F	E♭	D♭	C	B♭	A♭	G♭
[F♯	E	D	C♯	B	A	G
[G♭	—	—	D♭	C♭	—	—
G	F	E♭	D	C	B♭	A♭
[G♯	F♯	E	—	C♯	B	A
[A♭	G♭	—	E♭	D♭	C♭	—
A	G	F	E	D	C	B♭
[A♯	—	F♯	—	—	C♯	B
[B♭	A♭	G♭	F	E♭	D♭	C♭
[B	A	G	F♯	E	D	C
[C♭	—	—	G♭	—	—	—

Since the modes are derived from major scales, you can use the seven major-scale fingering types to play modal scales. The charts that follow provide the position and fingering type used to play scales in every modal key. Take the time to develop your own modal scale patterns using the charts in this section. This will improve your ability to transpose modal scales on the spot—and to improvise freely using these interesting and evocative scale forms.

Dorian Scale Positions

Key			Fingering Type				
	1	2	3	4	5	6	7
C	XII	X	IX	VII	V	III	II
C♯ (D♭)	XIII	XI	X	VIII	VI	IV	III
D	II	XII	XI	IX	VII	V	IV
E♭ (D♯)	III	I	XII	X	VIII	VI	V
E	IV	II	XIII	XI	IX	VII	VI
F	V	III	II	XII	X	VIII	VII
F♯	VI	IV	III	XIII	XI	IX	VIII
G	VII	V	IV	II	XII	X	IX
A♭ (G♯)	VIII	VI	V	III	I	XI	X
A	IX	VII	VI	IV	II	XII	XI
B♭	X	VIII	VII	V	III	I	XII
B	XI	IX	VIII	VI	IV	II	XIII

Phrygian Scale Positions

Key			Fingering Type				
	1	2	3	4	5	6	7
C	X	VIII	VII	V	III	I	XII
C♯	XI	IX	VIII	VI	IV	II	XIII
D	XII	X	IX	VII	V	III	II
E♭ (D♯)	XIII	XI	X	VIII	VI	IV	III
E	II	XII	XI	IX	VII	V	IV
F (E♯)	III	I	XII	X	VIII	VI	V
F♯	IV	II	XIII	XI	IX	VII	VI
G	V	III	II	XII	X	VIII	VII
G♯	VI	IV	III	XIII	XI	IX	VIII
A	VII	V	IV	II	XII	X	IX
B♭ (A♯)	VIII	VI	V	III	I	XI	X
B	IX	VII	VI	IV	II	XII	XI

Lydian Scale Positions

Key			Fingering Type				
	1	2	3	4	5	6	7
C	IX	VII	VI	IV	II	XII	XI
D♭	X	VIII	VII	V	III	I	XII
D	XI	IX	VIII	VI	IV	II	XIII
E♭	XII	X	IX	VII	V	III	II
E (F♭)	XIII	XI	X	VIII	VI	IV	III
F	II	XII	XI	IX	VII	V	IV
G♭ (F♯)	III	I	XII	X	VIII	VI	V
G	IV	II	XIII	XI	IX	VII	VI
A♭	V	III	II	XII	X	VIII	VII
A	VI	IV	III	XIII	XI	IX	VIII
B♭	VII	V	IV	II	XII	X	IX
C♭ (B)	VIII	VI	V	III	I	XI	X

Mixolydian Scale Positions

Key			Fingering Type				
	1	2	3	4	5	6	7
C	VII	V	IV	II	XII	X	IX
Db (C#)	VIII	VI	V	III	I	XI	X
D	IX	VII	VI	IV	II	XII	XI
Eb	X	VIII	VII	V	III	I	XII
E	XI	IX	VIII	VI	IV	II	XIII
F	XII	X	IX	VII	V	III	II
F# (Gb)	XIII	XI	X	VIII	VI	IV	III
G	II	XII	XI	IX	VII	V	IV
Ab (G#)	III	I	XII	X	VIII	VI	V
A	IV	II	XIII	XI	IX	VII	VI
Bb	V	III	II	XII	X	VIII	VII
B	VI	IV	III	XIII	XI	IX	VIII

Aeolian Scale Positions

Key			Fingering Type				
	1	2	3	4	5	6	7
C	V	III	II	XII	X	VIII	VII
C#	VI	IV	III	XIII	XI	IX	VIII
D	VII	V	IV	II	XII	X	IX
Eb (D#)	VIII	VI	V	III	I	XI	X
E	IX	VII	VI	IV	II	XII	XI
F	X	VIII	VII	V	III	I	XII
F#	XI	IX	VIII	VI	IV	II	XIII
G	XII	X	IX	VII	V	III	II
G# (Ab)	XIII	XI	X	VIII	VI	IV	III
A	II	XII	XI	IX	VII	V	IV
Bb (A#)	III	I	XII	X	VIII	VI	V
B	IV	II	XIII	XI	IX	VII	VI

Locrian Scale Positions

Key			Fingering Type				
	1	2	3	4	5	6	7
C (B#)	III	I	XII	X	VIII	VI	V
C#	IV	II	XIII	XI	IX	VII	VI
D	V	III	II	XII	X	VIII	VII
D#	VI	IV	III	XIII	XI	IX	VIII
E	VII	V	IV	II	XII	X	IX
F (E#)	VIII	VI	V	III	I	XI	X
F#	IX	VII	VI	IV	II	XII	XI
G	X	VIII	VII	V	III	I	XII
G#	XI	IX	VIII	VI	IV	II	XIII
A	XII	X	IX	VII	V	III	II
A# (Bb)	I	XI	X	VIII	VI	IV	III
B	II	XII	XI	IX	VII	V	IV

Another (and perhaps more practical) way of transposing a modal scale is to think of it as a variation of the parallel major (or natural minor) scale, as follows.

Dorian	Minor scale with raised 6th
Phrygian	Minor scale with lowered 2nd
Lydian	Major scale with raised 4th
Mixolydian	Major scale with lowered 7th
Locrian	Minor scale with lowered 5th and 2nd

If you know your major and minor scale fingerings, you will find it easy to adapt them to play modal scales in this way. For example, to play an F Lydian Scale, use an F major scale with a raised 4th.

F Major, Type 4

F Lydian, Type 4 (modified)

This *parallel* (or *tonic*) method of transposing modes is often easier and quicker than basing the modal scale on its relative major scale fingering. However, it is important to understand both of these methods of transposing modal scales.

Lydian Flat-Seven Scale

You are already familiar with the Lydian scale, built on the fourth degree of the major scale. The *Lydian flat-seven* scale is a useful variation commonly heard in jazz music. The Lydian flat-seven scale is generally used for soloing over dominant seventh chords (other than the V chord of the progression, for which the Mixolydian scale usually suffices).

The formula of the scale reveals it to be a cross between a Mixolydian and a Lydian scale, containing a flatted seventh and a sharped fourth (as compared to a major scale). This scale may also be thought of as the Lydian mode of the jazz melodic minor.

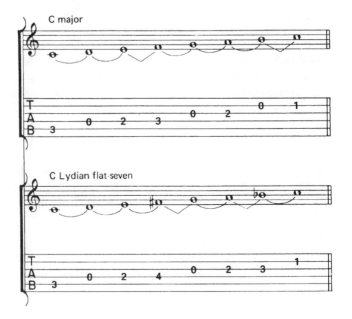

Lydian Flat-Seven Scale Patterns

Here are two handy, in-position patterns for the Lydian flat-seven scale, one with the root on the fifth string and one with the root on the sixth string.

THE CHROMATIC SCALE

The *chromatic* scale is the simplest example of a type of scale known as a *symmetrical* scale. The formula for a chromatic scale is simply all half steps. Because the intervals between notes are all identical, any note in the scale may be considered its root:

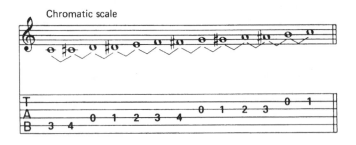

Chromatic Scale Patterns

The chromatic scale is not commonly used for improvising. However, since every type of music uses chromatic passages from time to time, the various patterns for this scale are well worth practicing.

PENTATONIC SCALES

In addition to the usual major, minor, and modal scales, there are many types of five-note scales called *pentatonic* scales. These scales occur frequently in both the major and minor modes.

Major Pentatonic Scale

The basic form of the pentatonic scale is the *major pentatonic*, which is often heard in Southern rock, rhythm and blues, country music, and light rock. This scale is built from the first, second, third, fifth, and sixth degrees of a major scale.

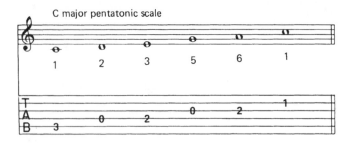

Major Pentatonic Scale Patterns

Here are four common major pentatonic scale patterns. Two are in-position and two feature position shifts (sometimes called "sliding scales").

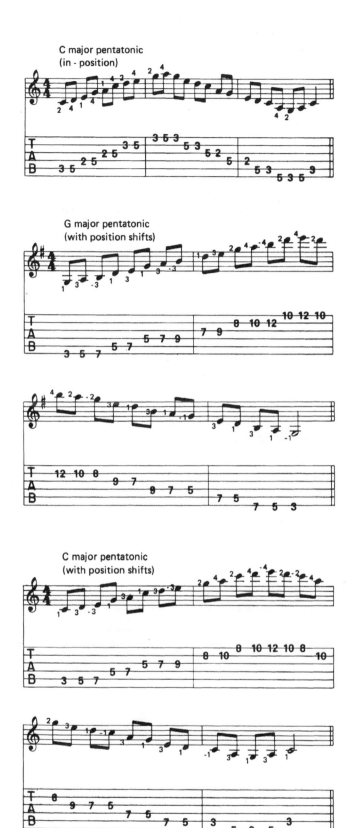

Minor Pentatonic Blues Scale

By taking the relative minor of the major pentatonic scale, you can produce a *minor pentatonic* scale (also called the *blues scale*). Thus the C major pentatonic scale becomes an A blues scale by starting it on A.

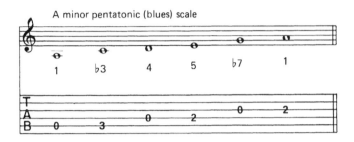

Minor Pentatonic Blues Scale Patterns

Here are four common minor pentatonic scale patterns, two in-position and two featuring position shifts.

Note that even the "sliding scales," are moveable, so you can play them in other positions on the neck to produce scales in different keys.

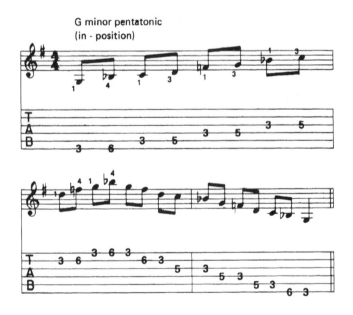

BLUES SCALE VARIATIONS

Blues and rock music sometimes features variations on the blues scale, including six-note and seven-note patterns.

Major Six-Note Blues Scale

The six-note blues scale (or *major blues scale*) below is based on the major pentatonic scale (with an added ♭3). The presence of a ♮3 in this blues scale gives it a "major sound."

C "Major" Six-Note Blues Scale

Major Six-Note Blues Scale Patterns

As with pentatonic scales, the four fingering types which work best for six-note (or *hexatonic*) blues scales are based on major-scale fingering Types 1, 2, 5, and 6, as shown.

Type 1

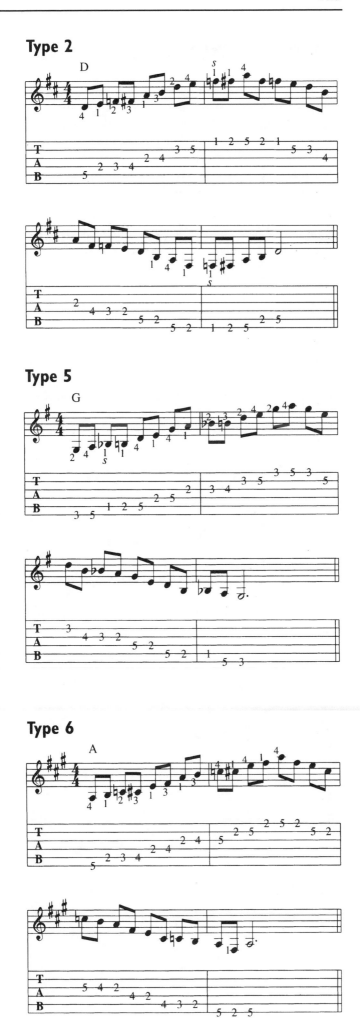

Minor Six-Note Blues Scale

Here is another popular six-note blues scale, which is formed by adding a ♭5 to the standard minor pentatonic scale. This "minor" blues scale contains the same notes as the scale above and is considered its relative minor.

A "Minor" Six-Note Blues Scale

To play this scale in any key, start on the sixth degree of the relative major blues scale and apply the same fingering. Try this now using the four fingering patterns above to play A, B, E, and F♯ "minor" six-note blues scales.

Seven-Note Blues Scale

The *seven-note blues scale* is another popular variation that is commonly heard in blues, jazz, and rock settings. This scale contains elements of both the "major" and "minor" six-note blues scales previously shown.

C Seven-Note Blues Scale

Seven-Note Blues Scale Patterns

Play this C seven-note blues scale exercise, which incorporates patterns derived from E♭ major-scale fingering Types 2, 1, 6, and 5. It is a common practice to reverse the second and third degrees of this scale when descending, as shown in this example.

DIMINISHED SCALE

Like the chromatic scale, the *diminished* scale is symmetrical. This means that more than one note in the scale may be considered the root. The formula for the diminished scale is a repeating alternation of whole-step/half-step. By starting on every other degree you can create three other scales with identical formulas. This means that the C diminished scale shown below could also be considered an E-flat diminished scale, a G-flat diminished scale, or an A diminished scale.

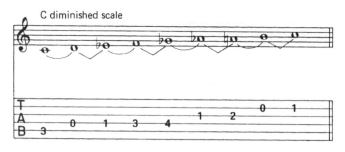

In addition to being used to solo over diminished seventh chords, the diminished scale is often used over dominant seventh chords to add tensions (flat-nine, sharp-nine, sharp-eleven, and thirteen). When used in this way, the root of the diminished scale should be one half-step above the root of the seventh chord.

Diminished Scale Patterns

Here are two common in-position fingerings and one sliding-scale fingering for the diminished scale. Remember that every other note may be considered the root, so practice these forms with different starting points to learn them thoroughly.

WHOLE-TONE SCALE

Another symmetrical scale is the *whole-tone* scale. Where the formula of a chromatic scale is all half steps, and that of the diminished scale is alternating whole and half steps, all intervals in the whole-tone scale are whole steps.

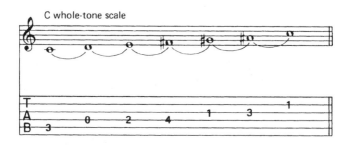

Whole-Tone Scale Patterns

This scale goes well with augmented seventh chords because it contains all the tones of the chord plus the ninth and the sharped eleventh.

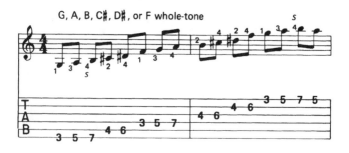

C, D, E, G♭, A♭, or B♭ whole-tone

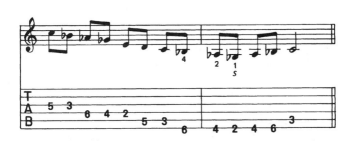

G, A, B, C♯, D♯, or F whole-tone

ALTERED SCALES

Combining the first half of the diminished scale with the second half of the whole-tone scale (one half-step above) yields the *altered* scale. This is used against dominant seventh chords altered with the tensions flat-five, sharp-five, flat-nine, sharp-nine, and/or sharp eleven.

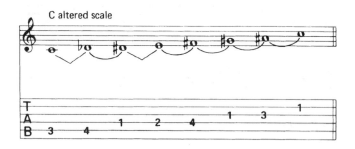

Notice that the formula of the diminished-scale portion of the C altered scale above shows it to be based on a D-flat diminished scale, even though it starts on C, a half step below. Notice also that while the diminished scale has eight steps per octave and the whole-tone scale only six, the altered scale has seven steps per octave just like the standard major, minor, and modal scales.

Altered Scale Patterns

Here are four good in-position patterns for altered scales.

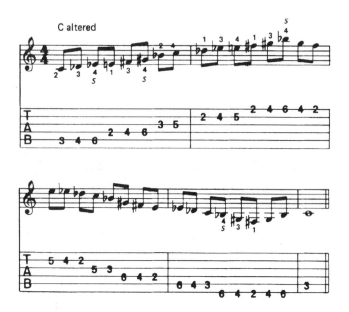

PENTATONIC SCALE VARIATIONS

A tonal pentatonic scale is a five-note scale that has no half steps. The most commonly used scale of this kind is the major pentatonic scale, covered previously in this book.

Tonal Pentatonic Scales

Four additional pentatonic modes may be derived from the major pentatonic scale by starting on each scale degree in turn. Here's a brief description of the tonal pentatonic modes. These scales occur in the music of many cultures and periods—from the ancient melodies of the Celts, Chinese, and Aztecs to today's most sophisticated rock and jazz improvisations.

Tonal Pentatonic Scale 2. Begins on the second degree of the pentatonic scale. This scale commonly occurs in "old-timey" folk music of the American Southeast. Contemporary bluegrass and country musicians often use this mode to evoke this haunting, traditional sound.

Tonal Pentatonic Scale 3. Begins on the third degree of the major pentatonic scale. Because of its ambiguous tonal center, this unusual scale has limited use.

Tonal Pentatonic Scale 4. Begins on the fourth degree of the pentatonic scale. This form is sometimes considered the "true" tonal pentatonic scale. It occurs in ancient music around the globe, but has limited use in usual contemporary settings. However, it can be heard in avant-garde, new age, and "world" musics that reflect African, Asian, or Celtic influences.

Tonal Pentatonic Scale 5. Also known as the *minor pentatonic scale* (or *pentatonic blues scale*), this form begins on the fifth degree of the major pentatonic scale. This scale is the basis for most traditional blues music—and naturally occurs in today's blues-based jazz and rock. This scale (along with its six-note and seven-note forms) is discussed more fully in the section "Blues Scale Variations."

D Tonal Pentatonic Scale 2

E Tonal Pentatonic Scale 3

G Tonal Pentatonic Scale 4

A Tonal Pentatonic Scale 5
(also known as Minor Pentatonic *or* Pentatonic Blues*)*

Because the tonal pentatonic scales may be used with a wide variety of chords and progressions, they allow for a good deal of melodic freedom. For this reason, modern songwriters and improvisers use these scales to evoke a powerful ethnic or avant-garde sound, particularly in an alternative jazz or new age context. Once you are familiar with the above scales, explore the modes derived from another major pentatonic scale in a different key, such as A or D.

Tonal Pentatonic Scale Patterns

You can derive fingerings for pentatonic scales from basic major-scale patterns. To play a major pentatonic scale, just leave out the fourth and seventh degrees of the parallel major scale fingering pattern. This fingering may also be used to play the four modes of the major pentatonic scale by starting on each scale degree in turn. Here are the four most useful fingerings for tonal pentatonic scales (based on major-scale fingering Types 1, 2, 5, and 6, respectively).

Type 1

Type 2

Type 5

Type 6

Semitonal Pentatonic Scales

A *semitonal pentatonic scale* is a five-note scale that includes half steps. Technically there are two such scales. The first one is produced by omitting the second and sixth degree of the major scale.

C Semitonal Pentatonic Scale

Like the tonal pentatonic scale, this semitonal pentatonic scale has four "modes," as shown.

E Semitonal Pentatonic Scale 2

F Semitonal Pentatonic Scale 3

G Semitonal Pentatonic Scale 4

B Semitonal Pentatonic Scale 5

Fingering patterns for semitonal pentatonic scales may be derived from major-scale fingerings. So, to produce the first semitonal pentatonic scale given above, omit the second and sixth degrees of the parallel major scale. This fingering may also be used to play the four modes of this scale by starting on each scale degree in turn. (As with tonal pentatonic scales, the four fingering types which work best for semitonal pentatonic scales are based on major-scale fingering Types 1, 2, 5, and 6.)

The second (or alternate) form of semitonal pentatonic scale is produced by omitting the second and fifth degrees of the major scale. Once you are familiar with this scale, try playing its four modes by beginning on each scale degree in turn.

C Semitonal Pentatonic Scale (Alternate)

As a general rule, semitonal pentatonic scales add a strong dissonant flavor to guitar solos and arrangements. These unusual scales (and their variations) are usually associated with the musics of specific cultures. For this reason, their harmonic applications depend upon their idiomatic contexts—and can not be discussed in general terms.

Several more interesting semitonal pentatonic scales are included in the section "Ethnic Scales" at the end of this book.

TAP-ON SCALES

A *tap-on* is basically a hammeron that is played with a finger of the picking hand. Most guitarists use the middle finger for tapping (indicated by a *T*). A tap-on is usually followed by a pulloff to the note below. This tap-on/pulloff sequence is then followed by another pulloff performed by the fretting hand. The resulting three-note pattern gives a triplet feel to tap-on riffs and scales. If you are interested in mastering this interesting technique, it really pays to practice scales that incorporate tap-ons in sequence. Below are two typical tap-on patterns for scales you have learned in previous sections of this book. Practice these examples, and then try coming up with your own tap-on patterns.

G Major Tap-On Scale

G Harmonic Minor Tap-On Scale

OPEN-STRING SCALES

Open strings create deep, natural-sounding tones which show off the guitar's resonant quality to its full advantage. For this reason, guitarists sometimes choose open-string scale forms, particularly for arrangements that call for a powerful and resonant sound.

By nature, open-string scales are not moveable. The scales that can be played in this way are limited by the fixed pitches of the instrument's open strings. Because of this limitation, there are comparatively few practical open-string scale patterns.

Since the fingerings for open-string scales are a bit more difficult than the usual positions, it really pays to practice them. If you play fingerstyle, you should have no trouble following the fingering indications (*p*=thumb, *i*=index, *m*=middle, *a*=ring). Pick-style players should use alternating pick and fingers, as shown.

Below are several typical open-string patterns for scales you have learned in previous sections of this book. Practice these examples, and then try coming up with your own open-string patterns.

Remember that the major and pentatonic scale fingerings may also be applied to the modes of the keys in which they are shown. For example, the D major pattern may also be used for an A Mixolydian or E Dorian scale—and the G major pentatonic fingering may be used for an E minor pentatonic blues scale.

D Major Open-String Scale

G Major Pentatonic Open-String Scale

E Aeolian Open-String Scale

A Minor Pentatonic Open-String Scale

G Whole-Tone Open-String Scale

SCALES WITH HARMONICS

Harmonics are often used in a solo context to evoke a haunting or introspective quality. Here is a G major pentatonic scale which will help you build your harmonic chops. This scale uses all natural harmonics played at the twelfth fret.

G Major Pentatonic Scale With Harmonics

You can play this scale in other keys by barring at any fret and using *artificial harmonics*. To play an artificial harmonic, lightly touch the string with the tip of the extended index finger of your picking hand at the point twelve frets above the fretted note. Then pluck the string with your thumb to sound the octave harmonic. Here are three more scales using artificial harmonics.

D Minor Pentatonic Scale With Harmonics

E Semitonal Pentatonic Scale With Harmonics

C Major Scale With Harmonics

ETHNIC SCALES

Many contemporary guitarists and composers have found inspiration by exploring the scales of other cultures, particularly those of the Eastern Hemisphere. You have already learned many important ethnic scales in previous sections of this book. For instance, tonal and semitonal pentatonic scales are found in the music of diverse ancient and modern cultures, from the native tribes of America and Africa to Indonesia and the Far East.

In this section, you will find additional ethnic scales which feature interesting "non-diatonic" harmonies. Certain of these scales traditionally feature microtonal harmonies which have here been interpreted for use with the standard guitar tuning. Although these scales may sound inappropriate in traditional settings, they can be very effective in contemporary new age and "world" music contexts.

Gypsy Minor Scale

The *Gypsy minor scale* (also called *Hungarian minor*) features a lowered 3rd and 6th, and a raised 4th. It may also be viewed as a harmonic minor scale with a raised 4th. This distinctive scale is common in the folk music of Eastern Europe and occurs in contemporary Turkish and Jewish music as well. During the 19th and 20th centuries, Béla Bartók and other composers devoted much attention to this interesting scale and its applications in contemporary classical music.

Neapolitan Minor Scale

The *Neapolitan minor scale* features a lowered 2nd, 3rd, and 6th degree—and may also be viewed as a harmonic minor scale with a lowered 2nd. This scale is identified with the *Neapolitan School*, a term loosely applied to an Italian style of composition popular in the 18th century.

Japanese Scales

Hirajoshi Scale

Kumoi Scale

In Scale

African Scales

Tanzanian Scale

Congolese Scale

Indian Scales

Bhairava Scale

Pooravi Scale

Marava Scale

Kanakangi Scale

Balinese Scale

Pelog Scale

4

Guitar Chord Dictionary

The versatile guitarist knows how chords are constructed—and can play a given chord in several different ways. Your choice of chord voicings is key to creating the style of music you want to play. Open tunings provide another palette of interesting sounds that can make your guitar playing sound down-home, foreign, or even otherworldly. In this book, you can learn how chords are built and named as well as how they are played in a variety of tunings.

The chord dictionary in this section is arranged according to the chromatic scale:

C—C♯/D♭—D—D♯/E♭—E—F—F♯/G♭—G—G♯/A♭—A—A♯/B♭—B

Several different positions are provided for each quality (major, minor, etc.) and alteration (seventh, ninth, etc.). This gives you a choice of where on the neck to play a particular chord and/or how the notes of the chord are arranged.

Basic Chord Theory

This section provides an introduction to basic chord construction. Here you will find the blueprints for many common guitar chords, with corresponding diagrams and symbols.

Three notes played simultaneously produce a *triad,* which is the simplest form of chord. (Two notes sounded together would be designated as an *interval.*) Understanding and playing chords will deepen your understanding of music as well as develop your musical ear.

Chord Diagrams

Chord diagrams, also called *chord boxes, chord windows,* or *chord frames,* make it easy to learn new chords. You will often see chord diagrams above the melody line in songbooks. A chord diagram shows you where to put your left-hand fingers on the strings of the guitar—and tells you the name of the chord you are playing.

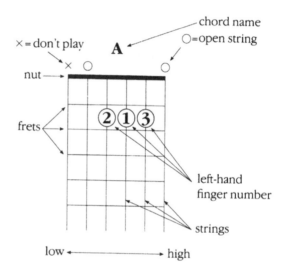

Major Chords

Let's take a look at some basic chord forms based on the note C. The *C major triad,* or *C major chord,* is formed by taking the first (or *root*), third, and fifth degrees of the C major scale. The chord symbol for this chord is simply *C.*

Chord Inversions

When the lowest note of a chord is not the root, the chord is called an *inversion*. The note that is on the bottom is said to be "in the bass." When the third is in the bass, the chord is said to be "in first inversion."

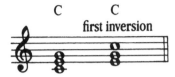

When the fifth is in the bass, the chord is said to be "in second inversion."

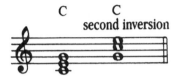

Sometimes a chord symbol will indicate what note is to be placed in the bass. This is done by separating the chord name and the name of the bass note with a slash. Thus, "C, first inversion" becomes "C/E"

Seventh Chord

A *C7 chord* (pronounced "C seven") is formed by simply adding a flatted seventh to the C triad.

Here are three different ways to play the C7 chord.

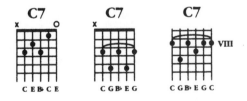

Minor Chords

If you lower the third of a C major chord by one half-step, you get a *C minor chord*. This chord is abbreviated *Cm*.

As with any chord, there are many ways to play Cm. Here are a few good voicings.

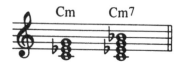

Minor Seventh Chords

Add the flatted seventh to the C minor chord and the *C minor seventh chord* results. The chord is abbreviated *Cm7*.

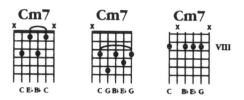

Augmented and Diminished Chords

An *augmented chord* is a major triad with a sharped fifth. The abbreviation for an augmented chord is a plus sign (+) or *aug*. A *diminished chord* is formed by flatting the fifth of a minor chord and abbreviated with the degree sign (°) or *dim*.

Diminished chords are usually embellished by the addition of the double-flatted seventh (°7).

Major Sixth and Major Seventh Chords

Major sixth and *major seventh chords* are often used in place of regular major chords. They are formed by adding the sixth or seventh degree, respectively, to a major triad. The symbol for a major sixth chord is simply the numeral 6. A major seventh chord is indicated by the symbol *maj7* or *M7*.

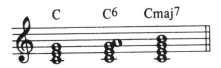

Table of Chord Symbols

Here's a list of chord types, together with the abbreviations found in common usage. The chords based on C are given as an example, but the equivalent relationships apply in all keys.

Symbol	Chord Name
C (C△)	C major C-E-G
CM7 (C Maj7, C△7, C7)	C major seventh C-E-G-B
CM9 (C Maj9, C△9)	C major ninth C-E-G-B-D
C6	C (major) sixth C-E-G-A
C6/9 (C9/6)	C sixth, add ninth C-E-G-D-A
Cm (Cmin, C-)	C minor C-E♭-G
Cm7 (Cmin7, C-7)	C minor seventh C-E♭-G-B♭
Cm6 (Cmin6, C-6)	C minor sixth C-E♭-G-A
Cm9 (Cmin9, C-9)	C minor ninth C-E♭-G-B♭-D
Cm7♭5 (Cmin7♭5, C-7-5, C∅)	C minor seventh flat fifth C-E♭-G♭-B♭
C7	C seventh, (C dominant seventh) C-E-G-B♭
C7sus4	C seventh suspended fourth C-F-G-B♭
C9	C ninth (C dominant ninth) C-E-G-B♭-D
C7♭5 (C7-5)	C seventh flat fifth C-E-G♭-B♭
C7♭9 (C7-9)	C seventh flat ninth C-E-G-B♭-D♭
C7♯9 (C7+9)	C seventh sharp ninth C-E-G-B♭-D♯
C11	for practical purposes = C7sus4
C13	C thirteenth C-E-G-B♭-(D)-A
C° (Cdim, C-)	C diminished C-E♭-G♭. For practical purposes, this chord does not exist in folk, pop, and jazz music. When you see this symbol, it is shorthand for C°7.
C°7 (Cdim7, C-7)	C diminished seventh. C-E♭-G♭-B♭♭ (=C-E♭-G♭-A)
C+ (Caug)	C augmented C-E-G♯
C+7 (C7+, Caug7)	C augmented seventh, C seventh augmented C-E-G♯-B♭

STANDARD TUNING

C Chords

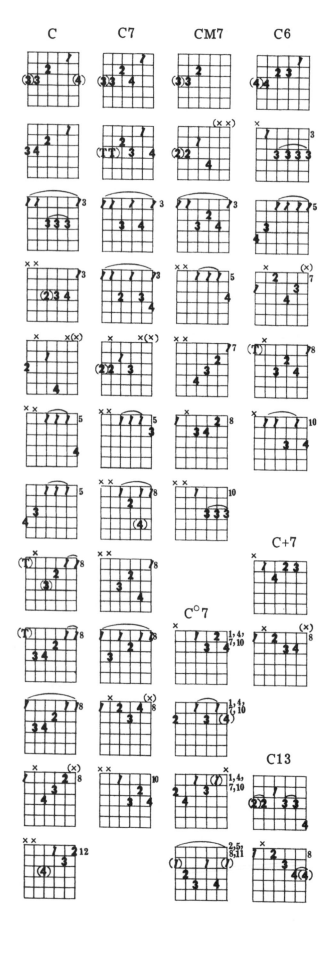

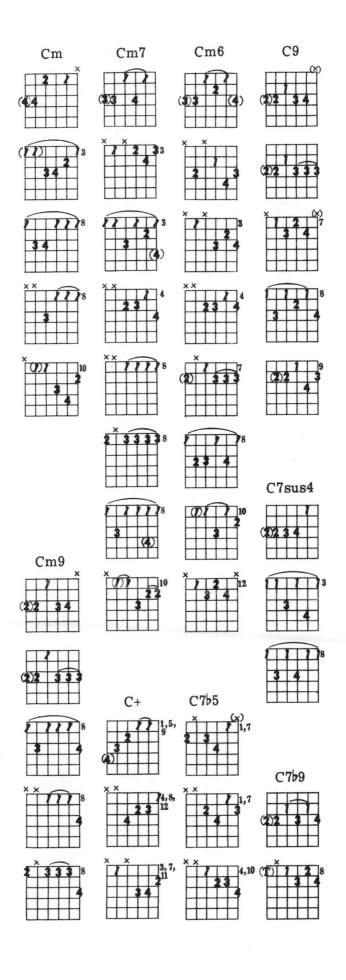

C♯/D♭ Chords

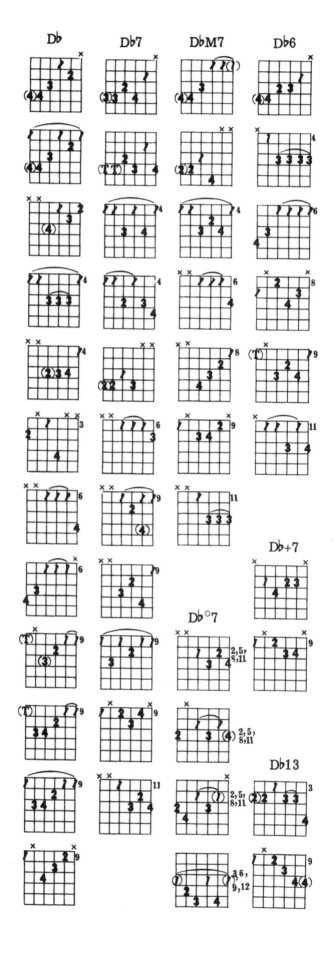

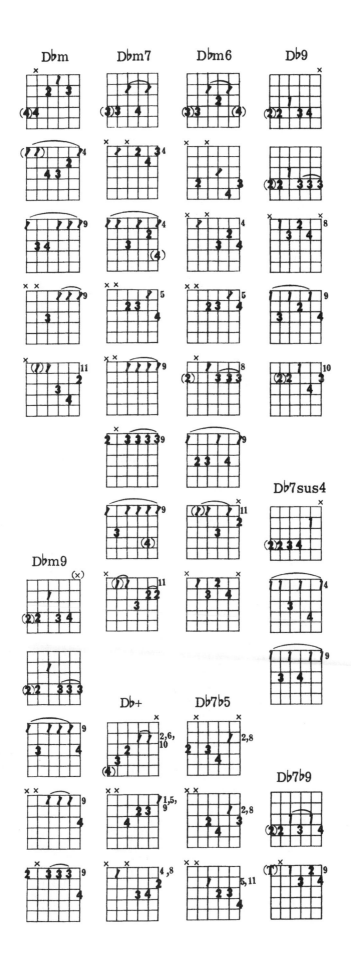

D Chords

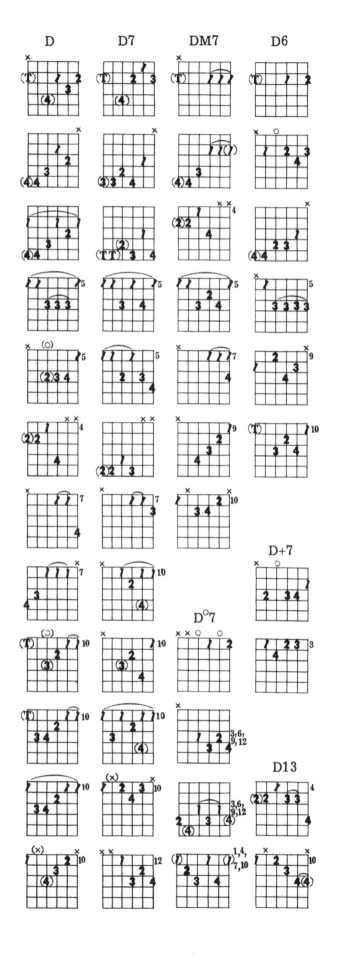

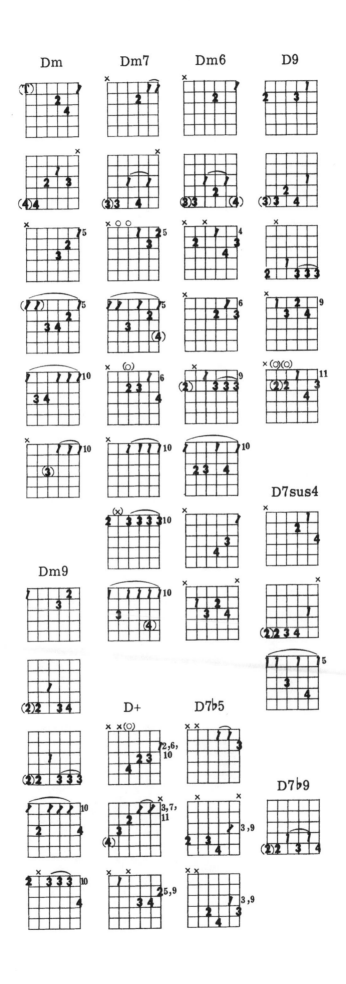

D#/Eb Chords

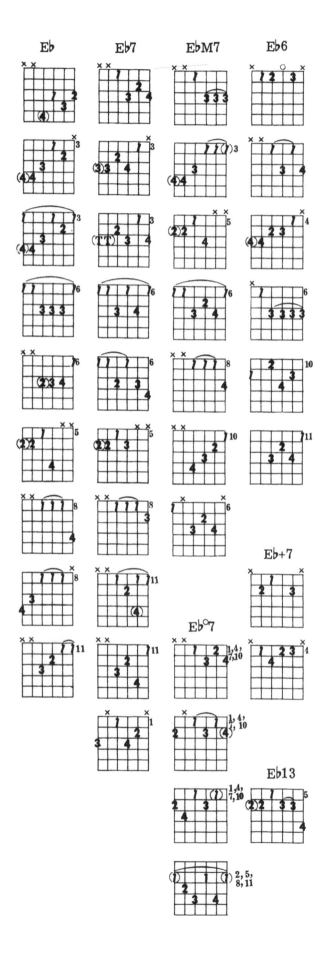

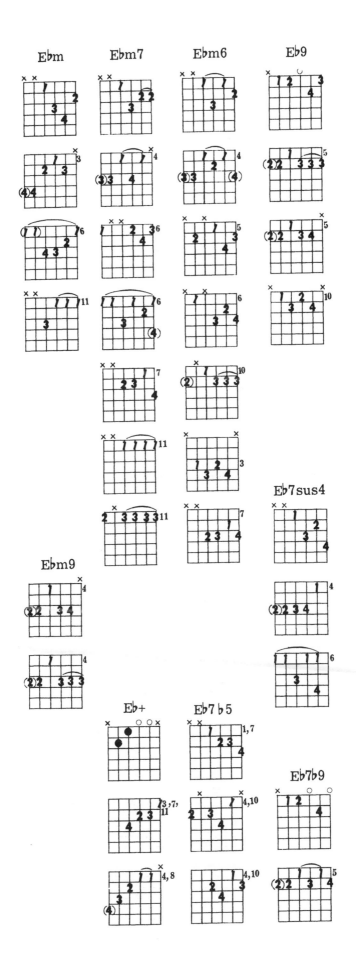

E Chords

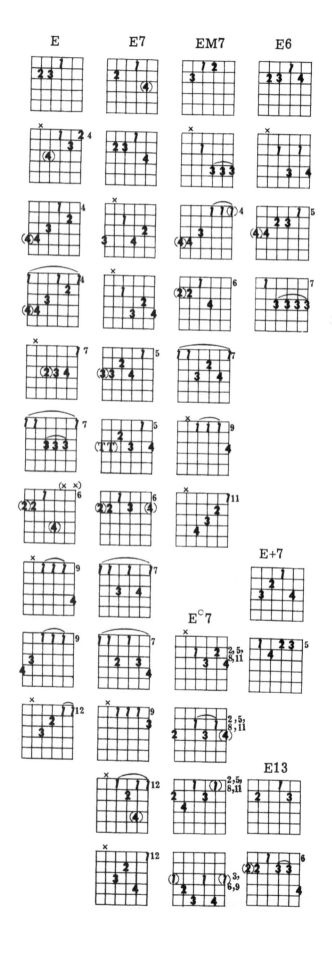

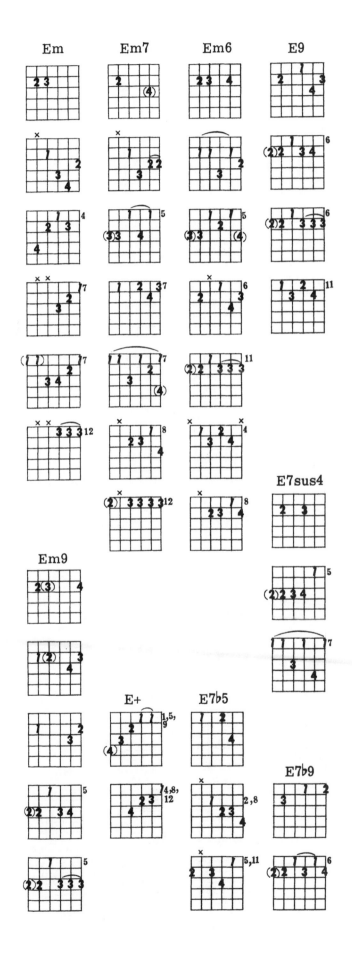

F Chords

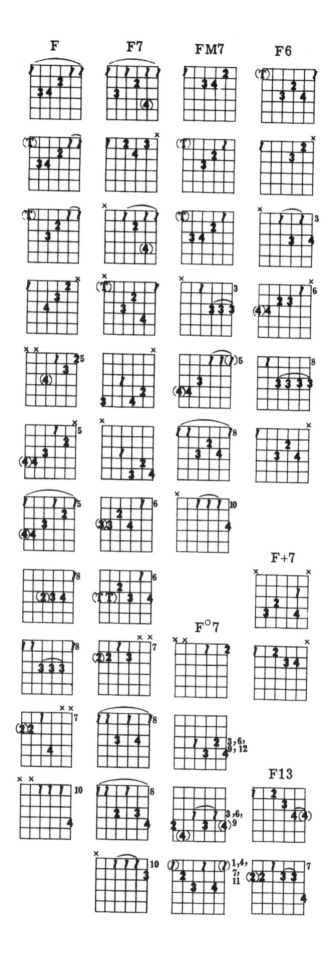

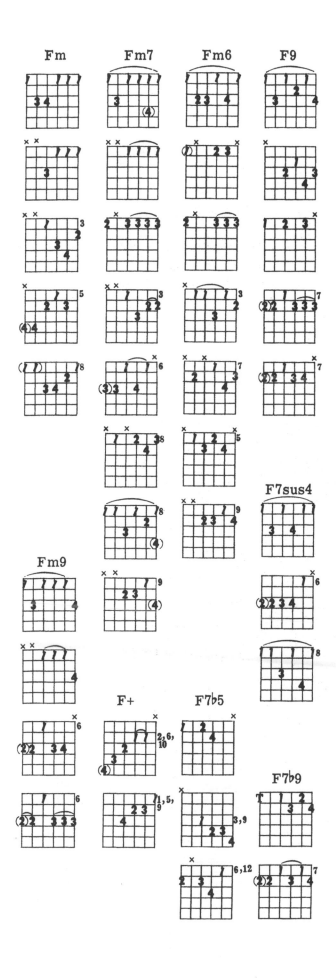

F♯/G♭ Chords

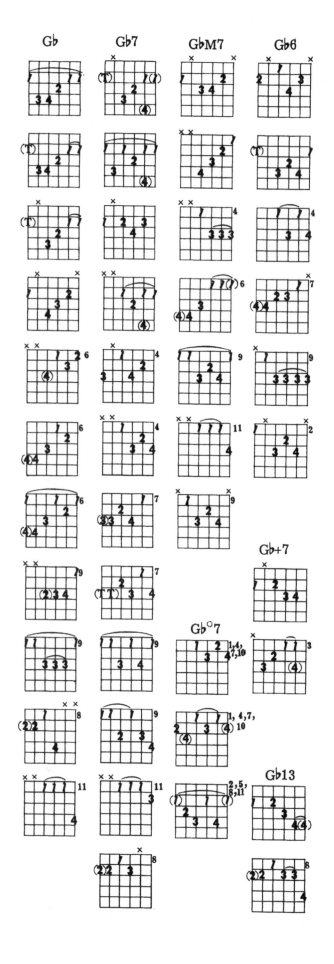

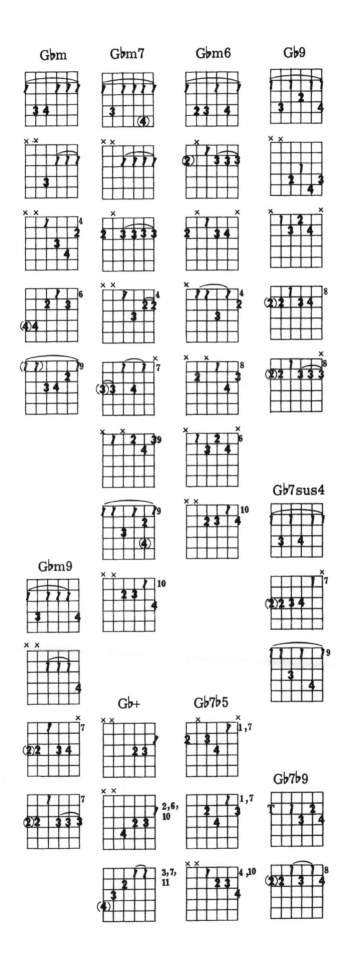

G Chords

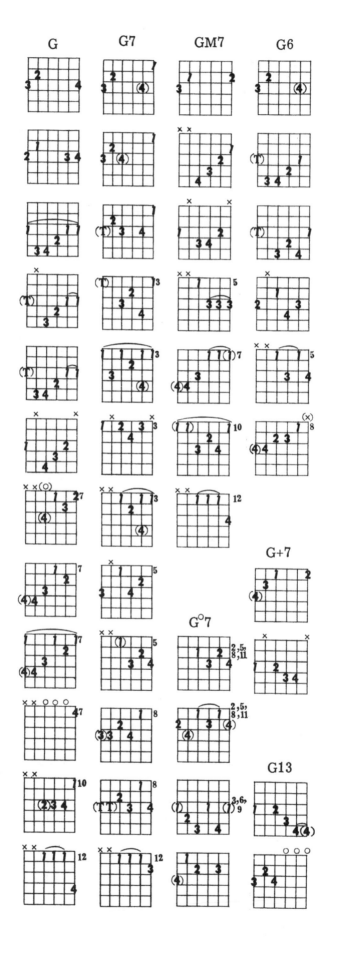

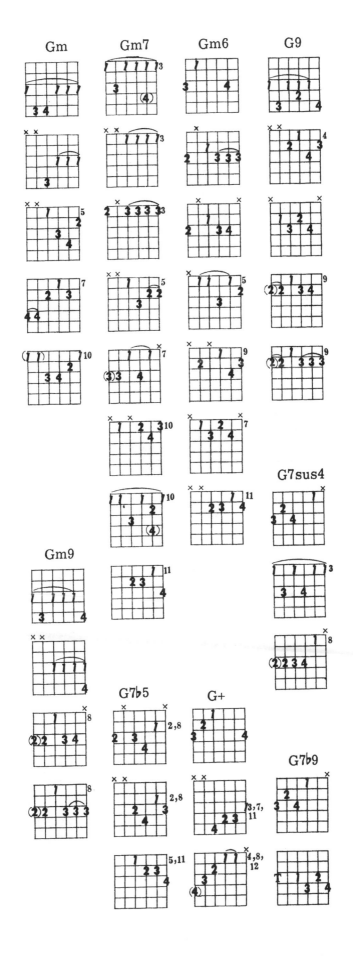

G#/Ab Chords

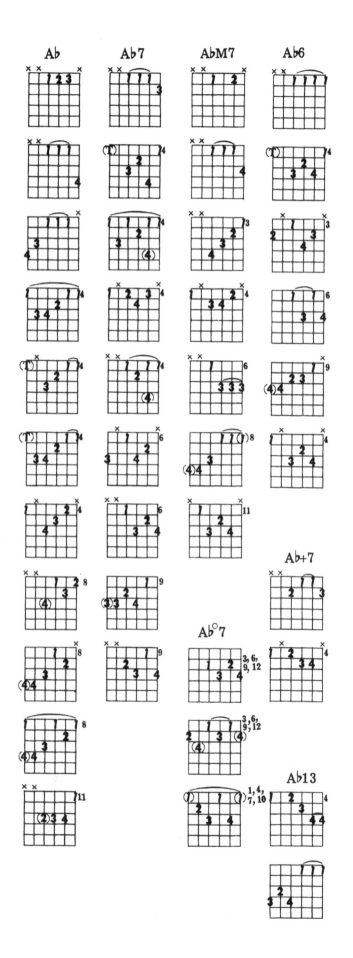

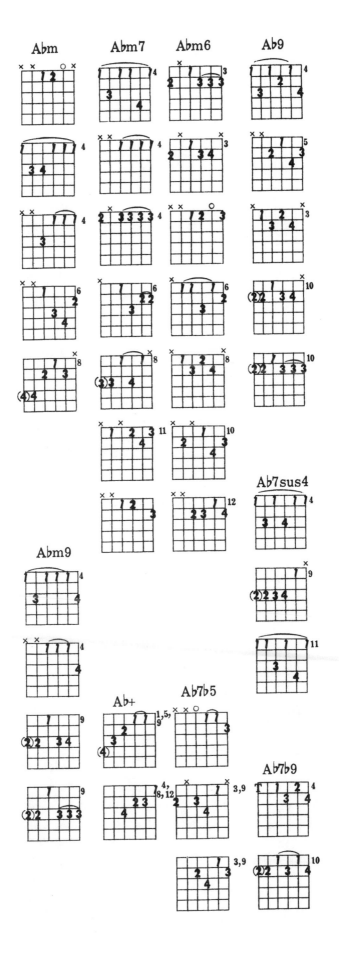

A Chords

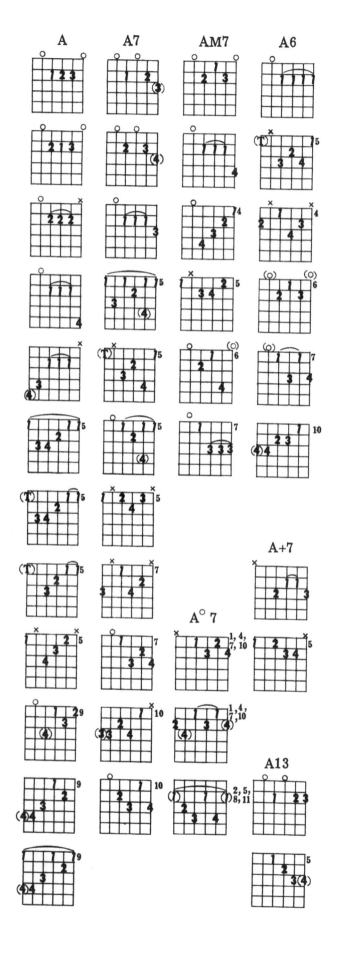

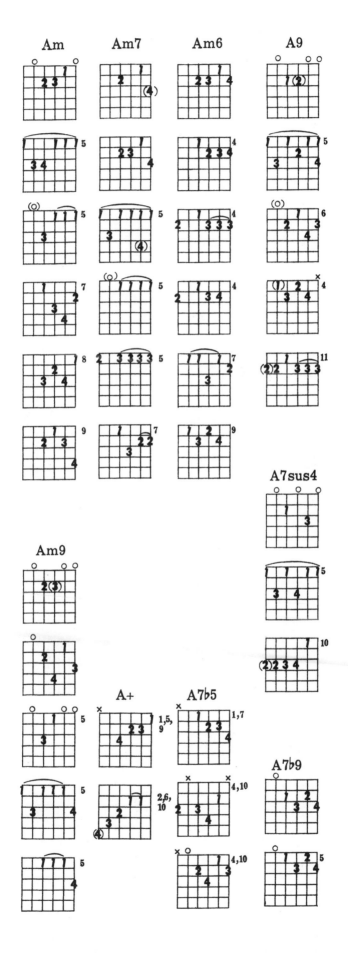

A#/B♭ Chords

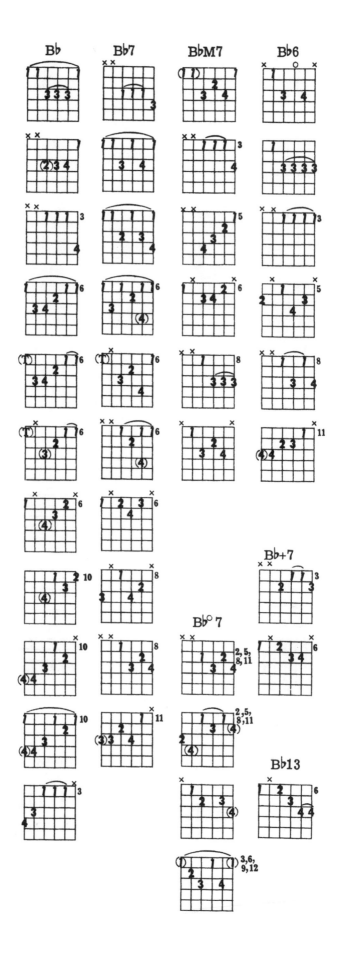

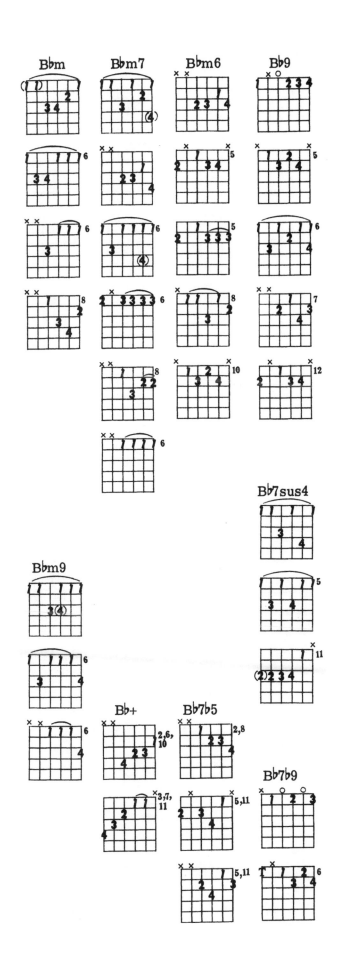

B Chords

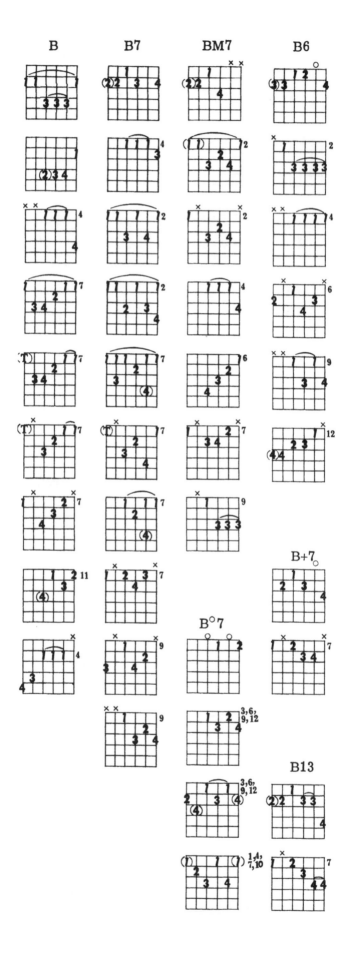

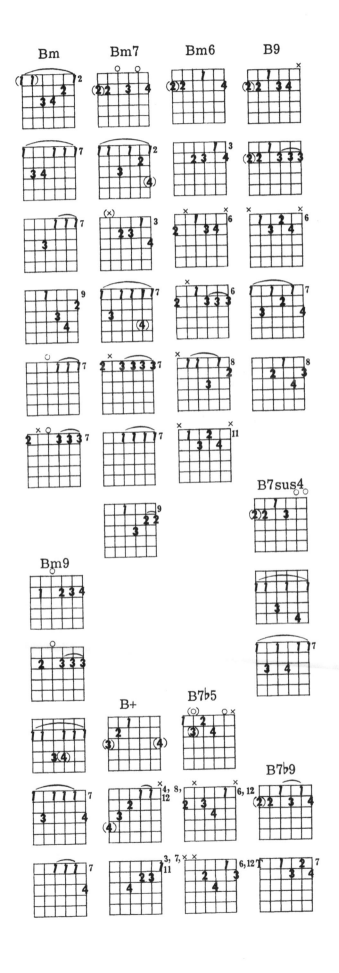

OPEN TUNINGS

The "standard" way of tuning a guitar—EADGBE—wasn't always the standard. This method evolved over hundreds of years, with input from several different cultures. However, many styles of ethnic and historic music are characterized by non-standard tunings. Alternate tunings also provide the contemporary guitarist with a rich palette of new sounds and effects. The sections that follow will give you a taste of the more common open tunings available to the guitarist, along with a selection of chord forms in each tuning.

Open G Tuning (DGDGBD)

For this tuning, the guitar is tuned to an open G chord.

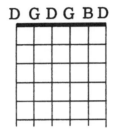

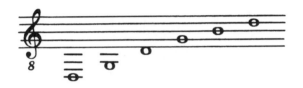

This versatile tuning corresponds to G tuning on the banjo. It is also sometimes called *Spanish tuning*.

Sometimes this pattern is used as an A tuning, with each string tuned one tone higher so that an open A chord results. In this case, the chords in the following diagrams should be named one tone higher (G becomes A, C7 becomes D7, and so on).

Chords in Open G Tuning

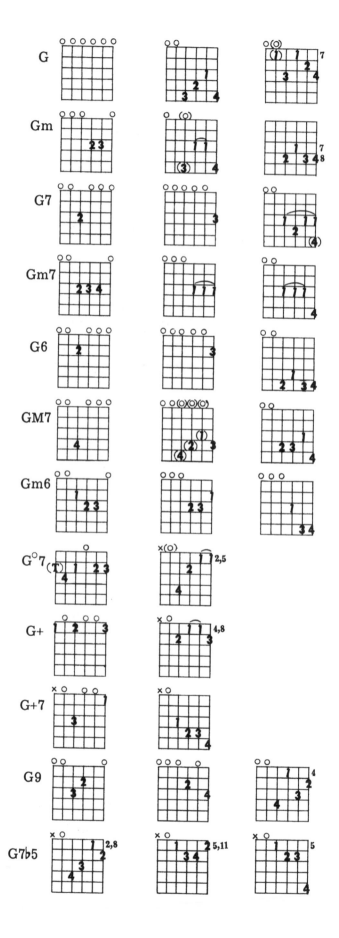

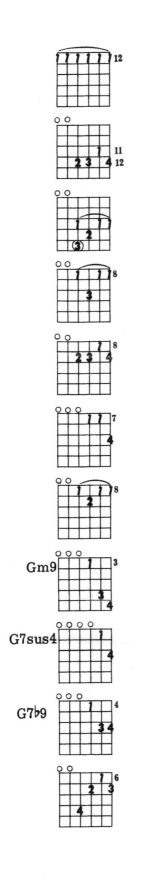

Chords in Open G Tuning

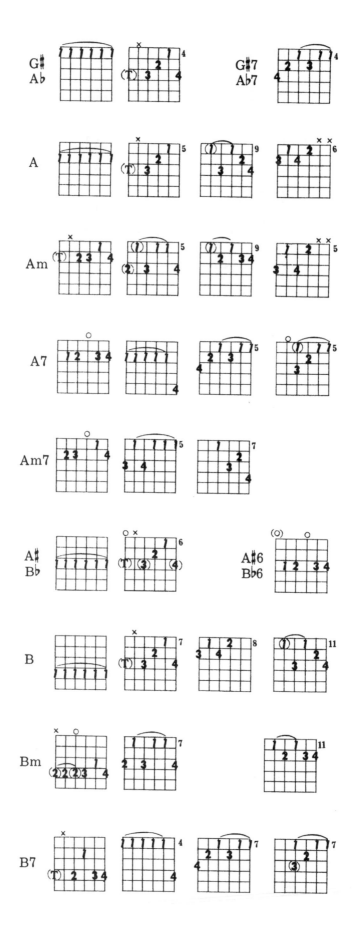

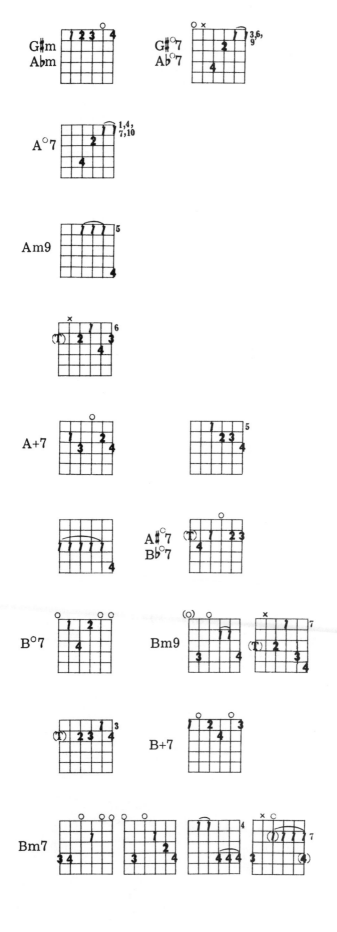

Chords in Open G Tuning

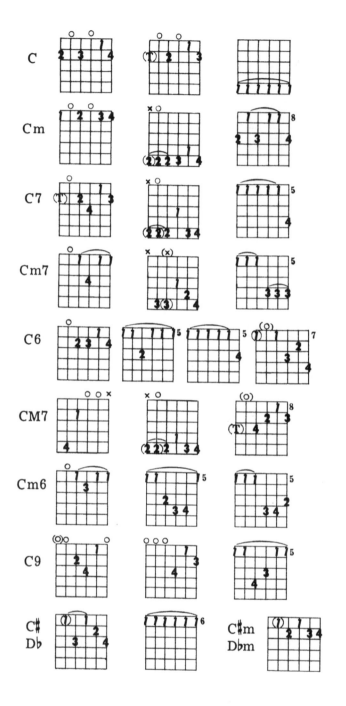

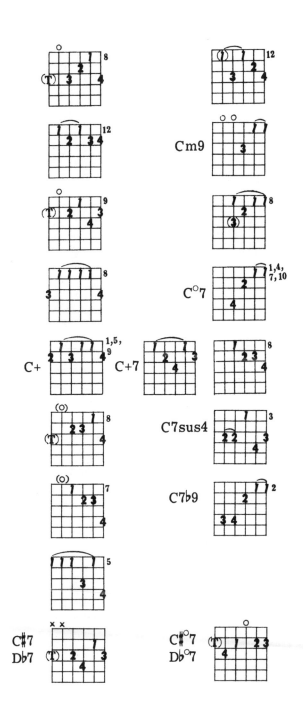

Chords in Open G Tuning

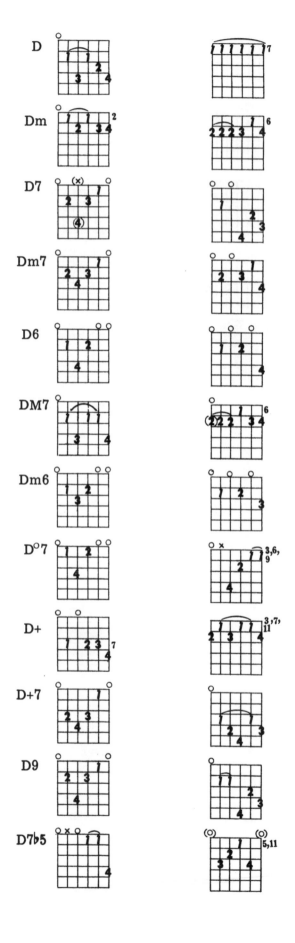

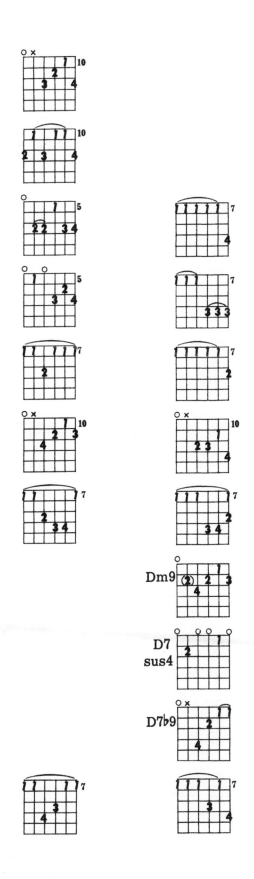

Chords in Open G Tuning

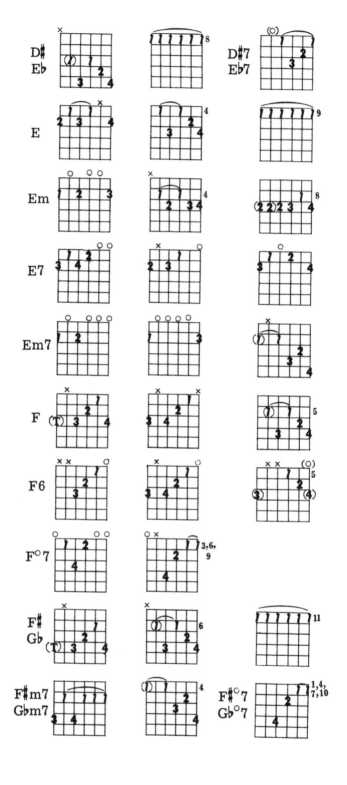

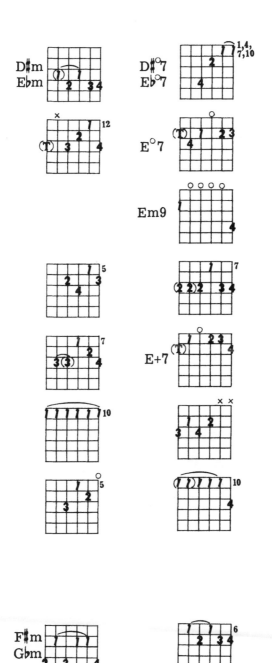

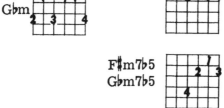

Open D Tuning (DADF♯AD)

This tuning is also known as *Hawaiian* or *slack key tuning*. It's also sometimes called *Vastopol tuning*, after a guitar piece entitled "Sevastopol," which was popular in the beginning of the twentieth century. Here the guitar is tuned to an open D major chord.

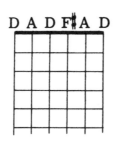

Open D is probably the most versatile of tunings, lending itself to just about any sort of song in any style, including slide and lap-steel styles.

Some players prefer to tune their instruments to an open E chord (EBEG♯BE) with each string one tone higher than in D tuning. This produces a brighter sound, since the strings are tighter, but it may be rough on your strings and on the neck of your guitar. If you use E instead of D, name the chords on the diagrams that follow one tone higher (D becomes E, A7 becomes B7, and so on).

Chords in Open D Tuning

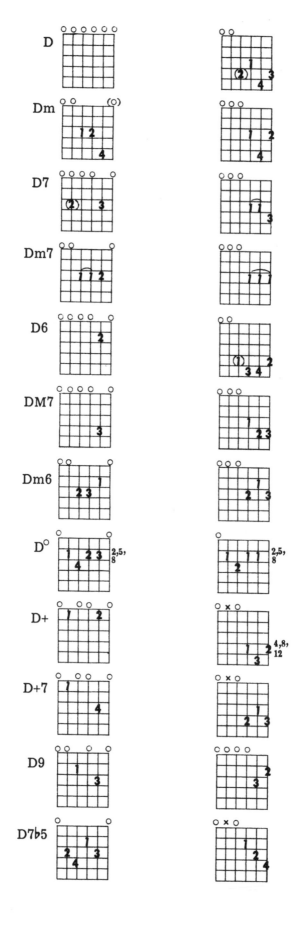

189

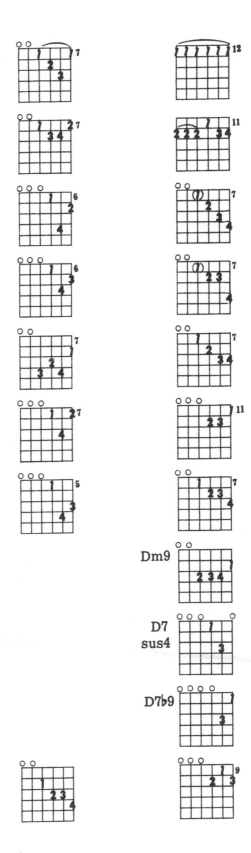

Chords in Open D Tuning

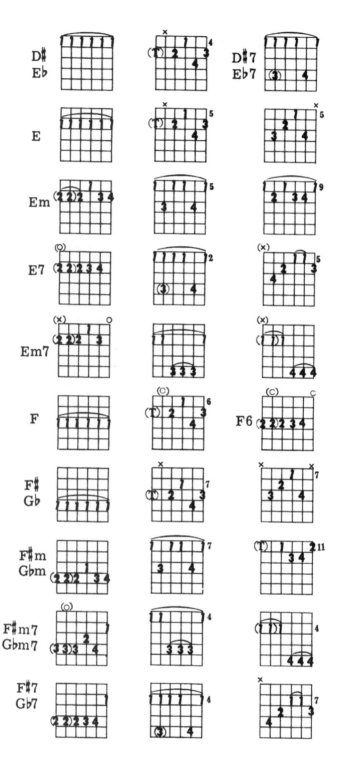

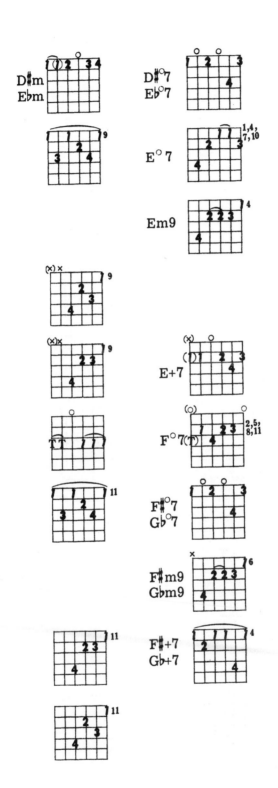

D#m
Ebm

D#°7
Eb°7

E°7

Em9

E+7

F°7(T)

F#°7
Gb°7

F#m9
Gbm9

F#+7
Gb+7

Chords in Open D Tuning

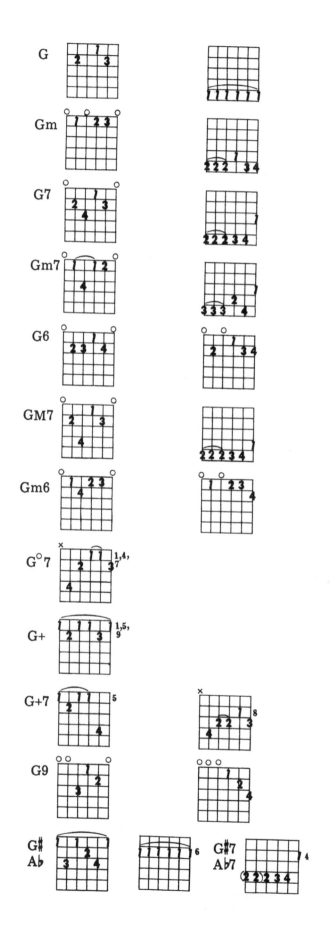

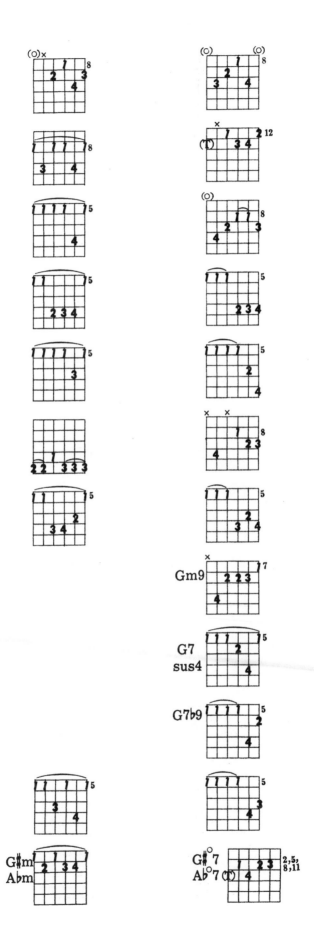

Chords in Open D Tuning

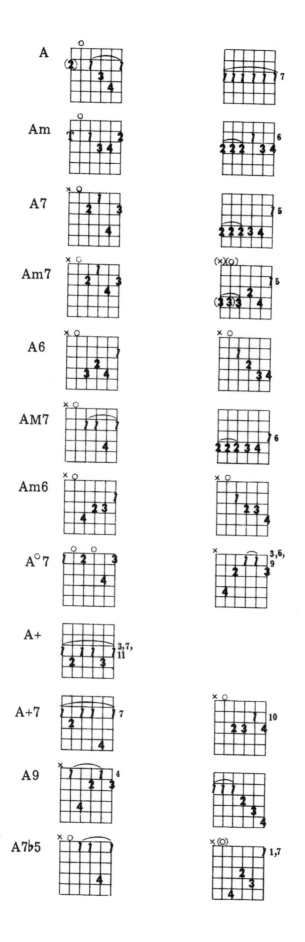

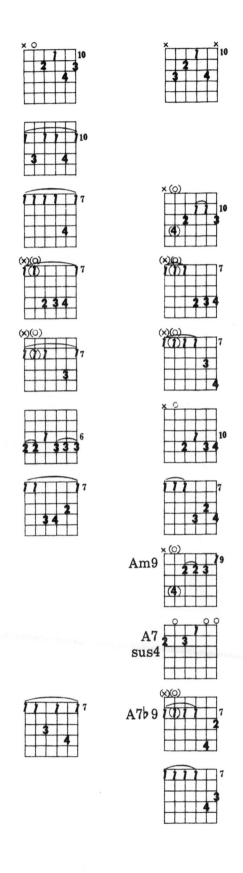

Chords in Open D Tuning

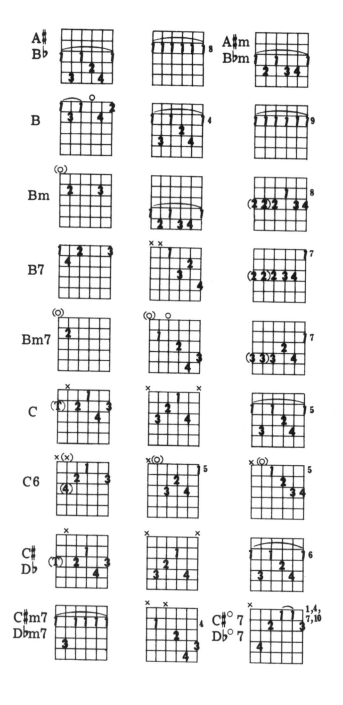

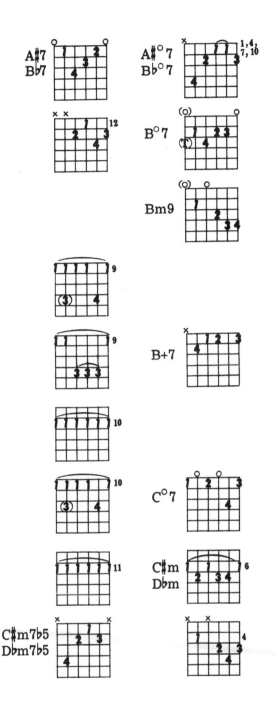

D Modal Tuning (DADGAD)

Here, the guitar is tuned to a D chord with a suspended fourth (and no third). The resulting sound has features of both major and minor modes. This provides a striking texture—at once modern and archaic. This tuning is rarely used by traditional guitarists, but is favored by modern guitarists, especially for bluesy sounds with very simple chord changes.

D A D G A D

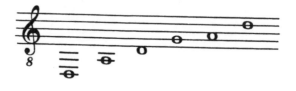

Chords in D Modal Tuning

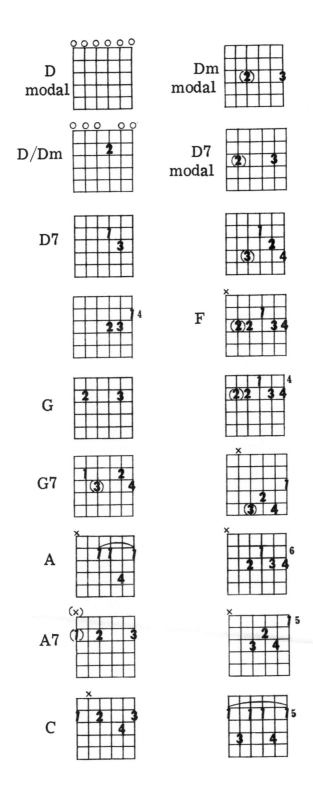

Dropped D Tuning (DADGBE)

This is the same as standard tuning, with the sixth string dropped one whole tone to D in order to facilitate playing in the key of D.

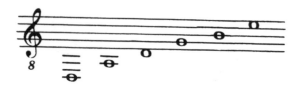

This tuning is particularly useful for fingerpicking styles that call for an alternating bass note pattern. You can use any standard chord shape with this tuning if you omit the sixth string. In addition, you can work out new fingerings by compensating for the two-fret drop of the sixth string. The most common chord fingerings are shown here.

Chords in Dropped D Tuning

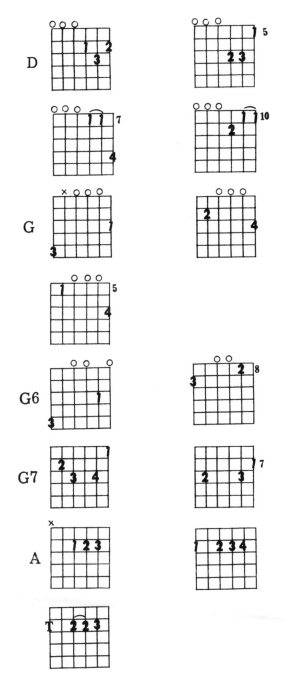

D Minor "Crossnote" Tuning (DADFAD)

Here the guitar is tuned to an open D minor chord, but the key played may be D minor or D major.

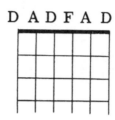

This tuning is called *crossnote* or *crosskey tuning* because the old-time bluesmen found it so effective for crossing over between minor and major tonalities. It also serves well for songs in minor keys with no blues tonalities.

Chords in D Minor Tuning

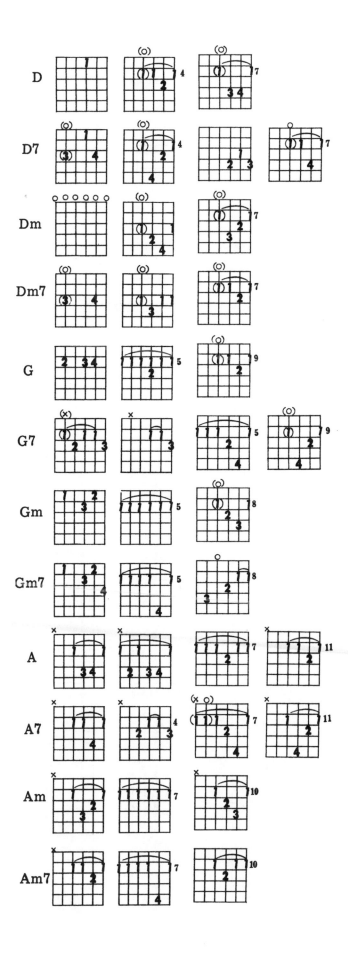

Open A Tuning (EAC♯EAE)

This tuning is especially useful for the Delta blues sound. Here the guitar is tuned to an open A chord.

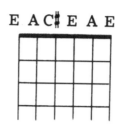

E A C♯ E A E

Chords in Open A Tuning

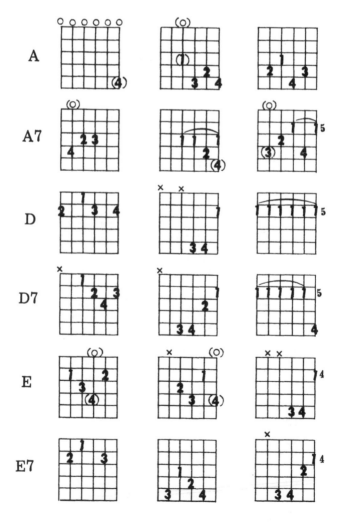

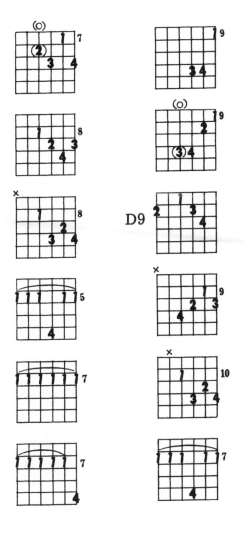

D9

Open C Tuning (CGCGCE)

This is a very beautiful tuning which is useful for a variety of different feels—from ancient to modern.

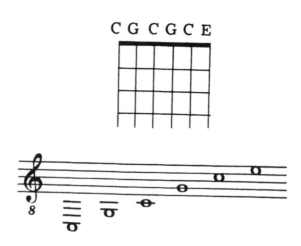

Chords in Open C Tuning

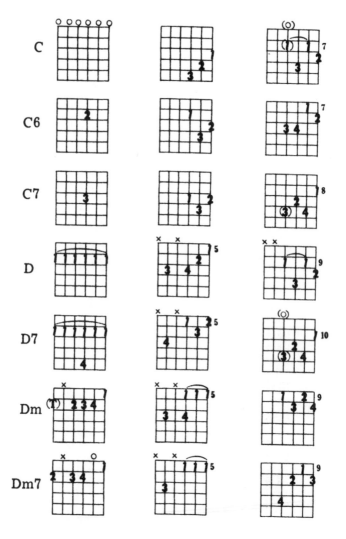

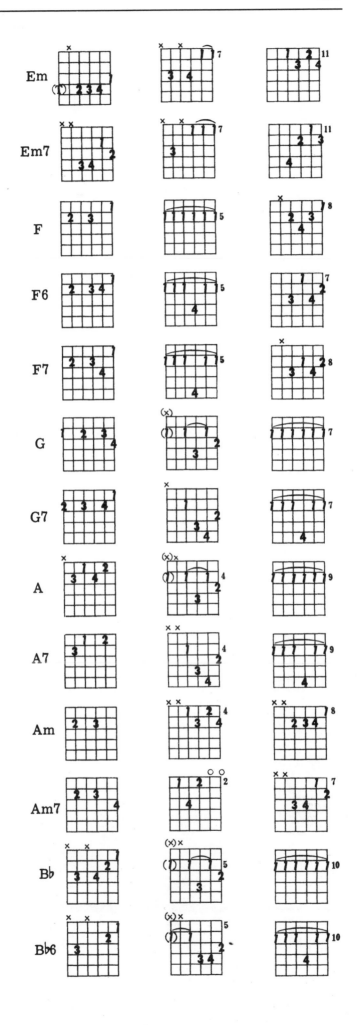

5

Guitar Manuscript Paper

This final book provides a supply of music manuscript paper especially designed for guitarists. This is a great place to jot down new chords, riffs, or complete songs or solos. If and when you run out of any of these three types of guitar manuscript paper, you can obtain more from your local music store. Just ask for Passantino guitar manuscript paper in the style you require.

Chord Diagram Paper. Use this type of paper to diagram chords and chord inversions. For a discussion on building and naming guitar chords, as well as information on chord diagram notation, see the section "Basic Chord Theory" in *Book 4: Guitar Chord Dictionary.*

Vocal/Guitar Tablature Paper. Use this three-line paper to write out songs for voice and guitar. You can add lyrics between the first and second staff, if desired. This paper is also useful for writing or arranging instrumental compositions for guitar and a solo treble instrument, such as flute recorder, violin, clarinet, or trumpet. For more information on writing music for the guitar and other instruments, see *Book 2: Music Theory for Guitarists.*

Guitar Tablature Paper. This two-line paper is designed for guitar solos of any kind. It provides a standard treble staff aligned with a guitar tablature staff with chord diagrams. For more information on writing music for the guitar, see the section "Guitar Tablature and Notation" in *Book 2: Music Theory for Guitarists.*

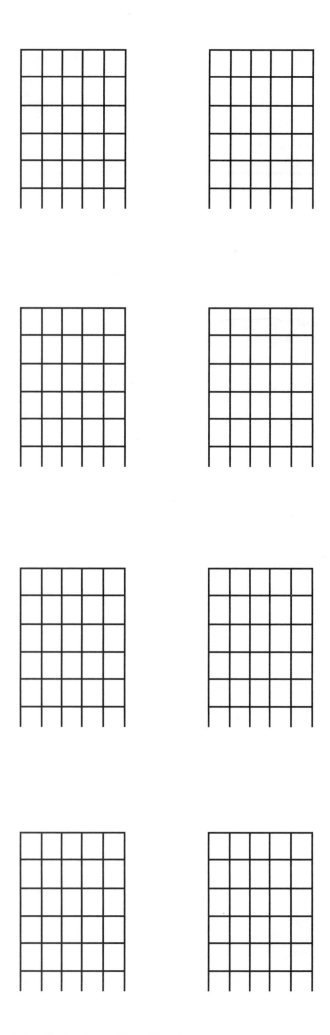

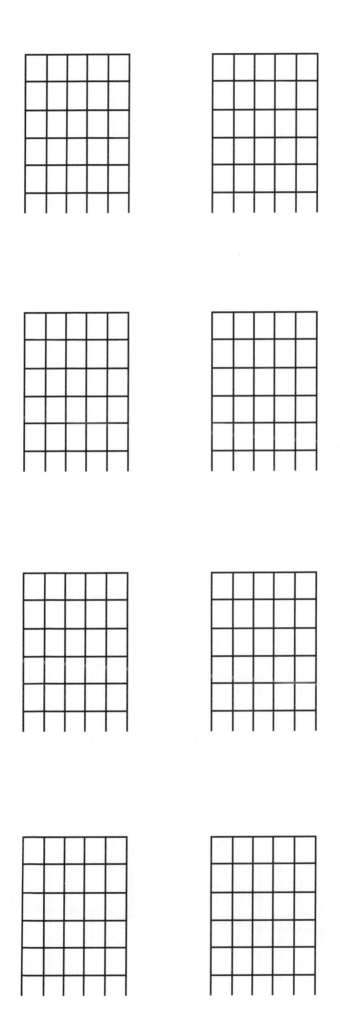

Chord Diagram Paper

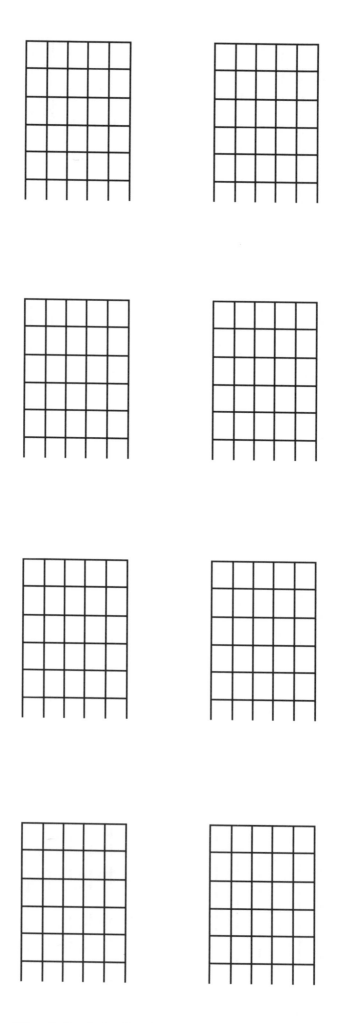

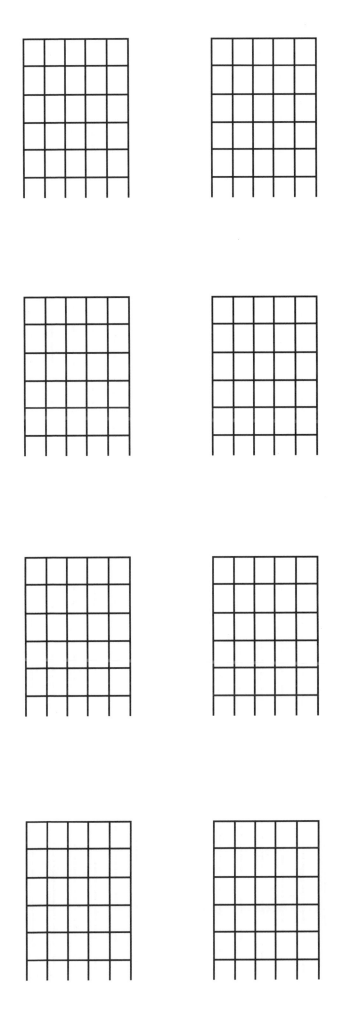

Chord Diagram Paper

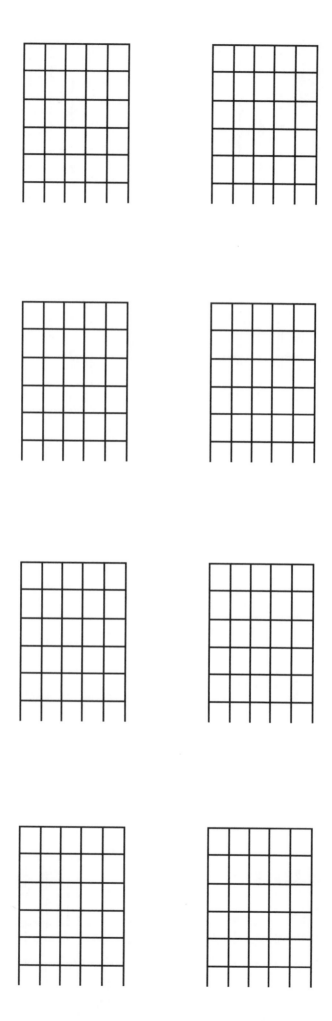

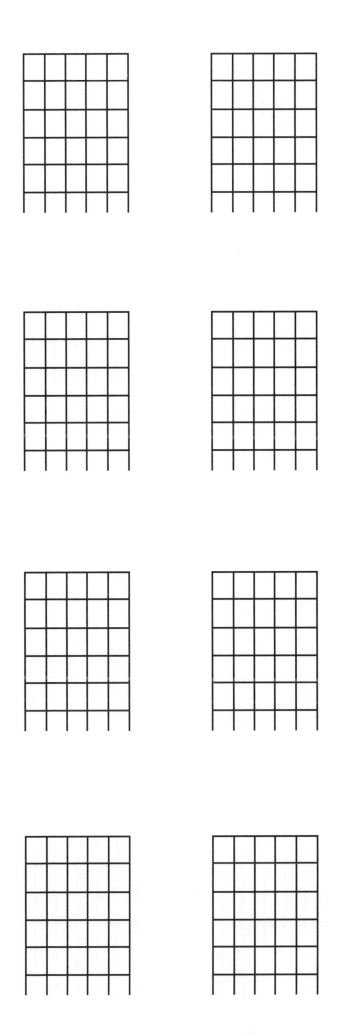

Chord Diagram Paper

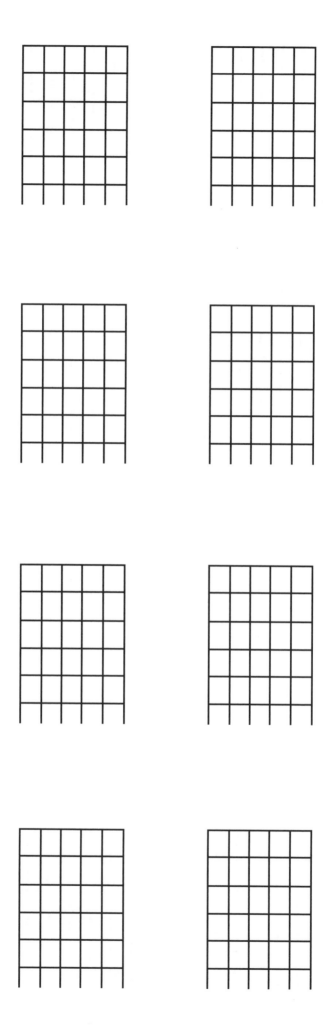

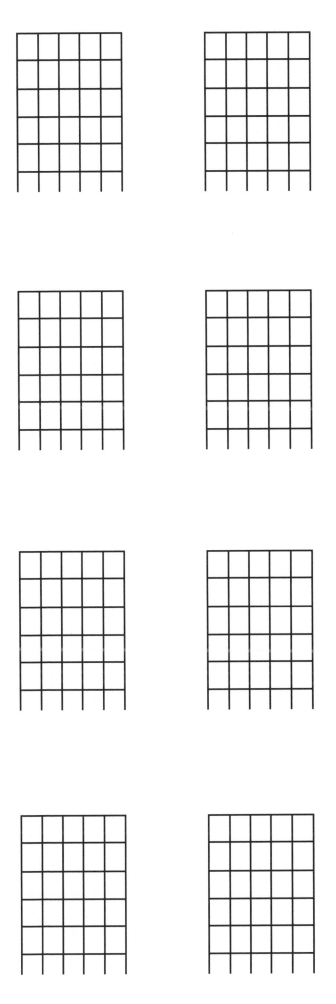

Chord Diagram Paper

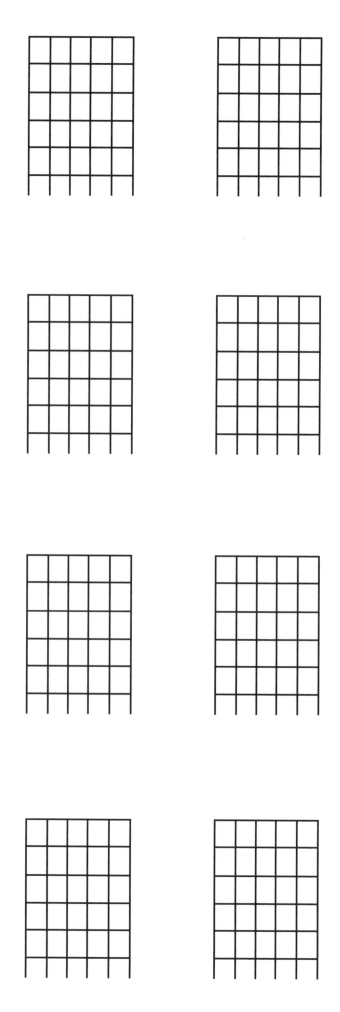

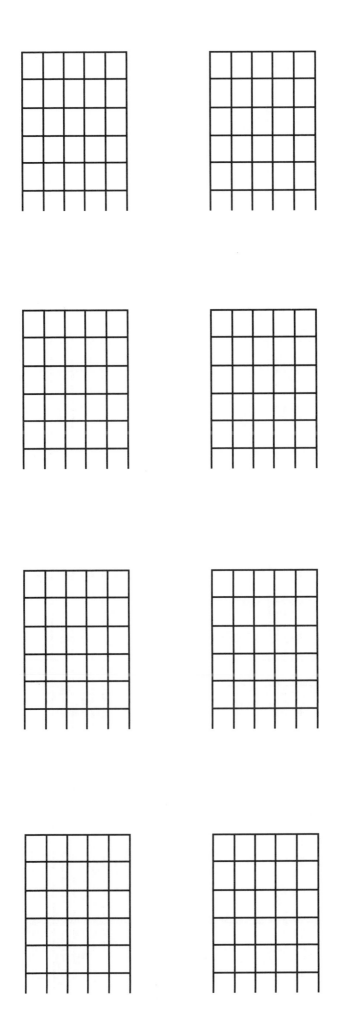

Chord Diagram Paper

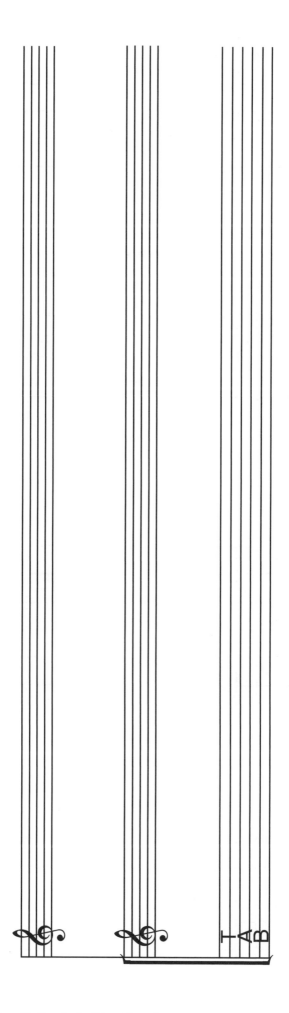

The Guitarist's Handbook

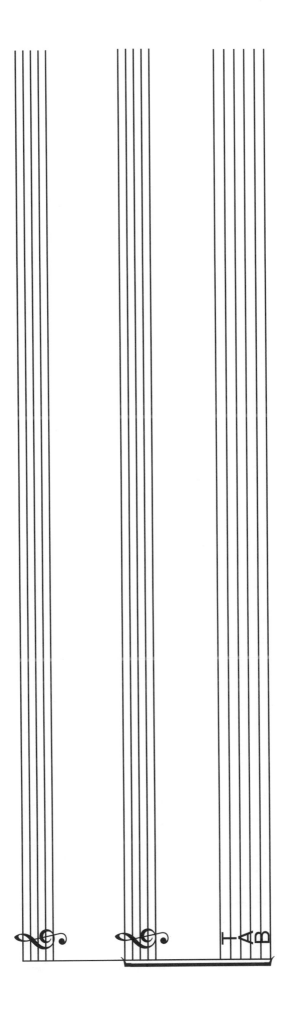

Vocal/Tablature Paper

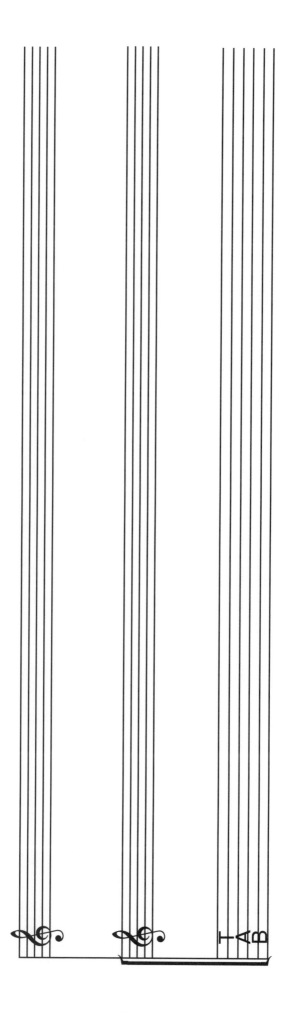

The Guitarist's Handbook

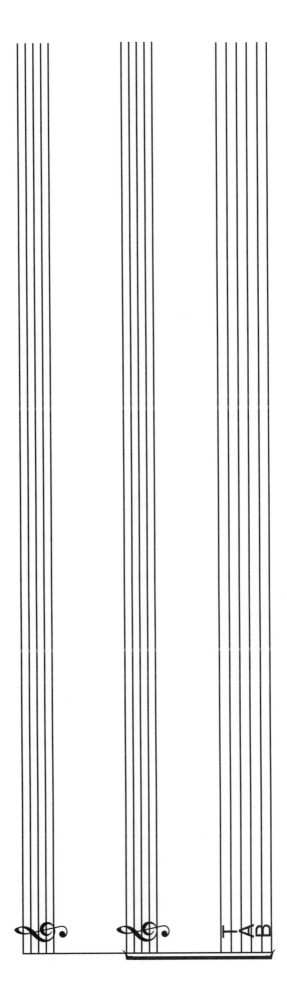

Vocal/Tablature Paper

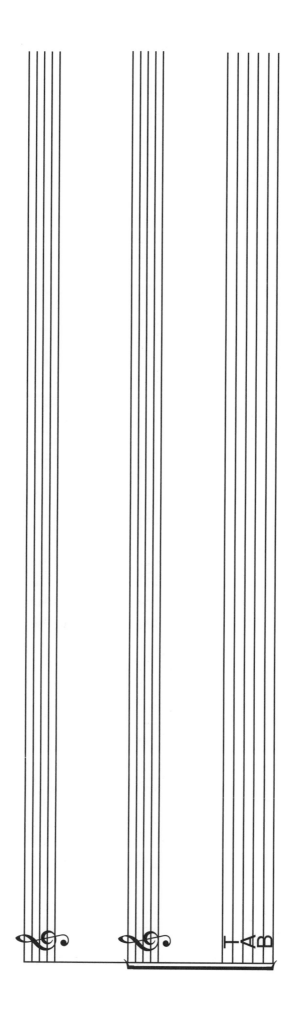

The Guitarist's Handbook

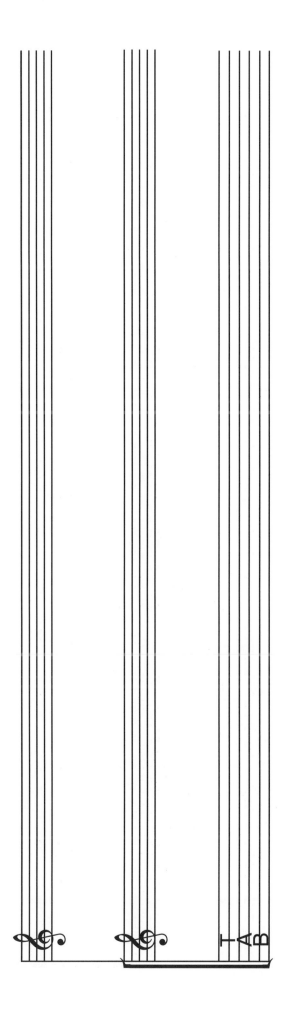

Vocal/Tablature Paper

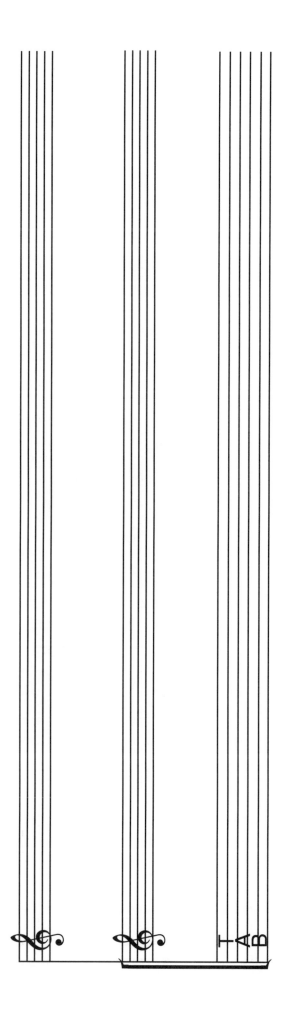

The Guitarist's Handbook

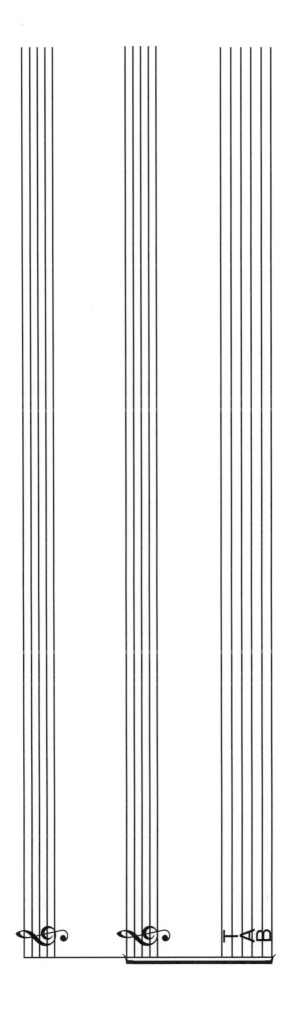

Vocal/Tablature Paper

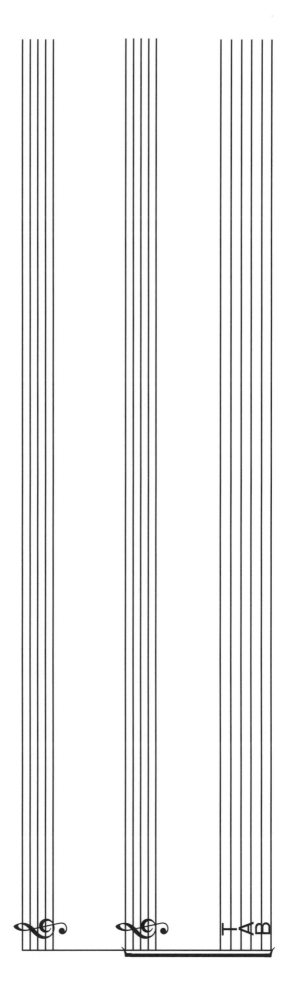

The Guitarist's Handbook

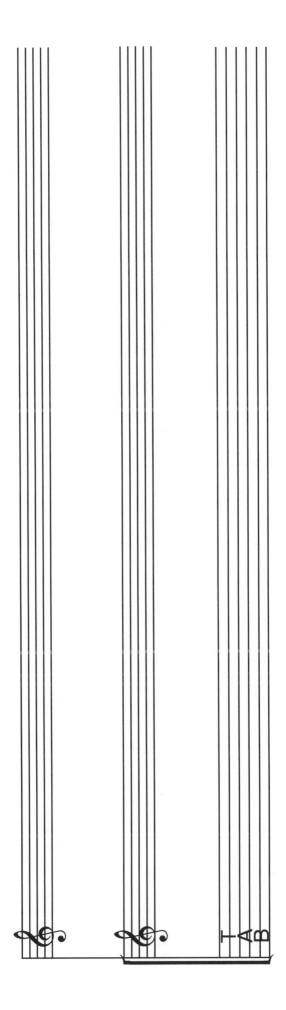

Vocal/Tablature Paper

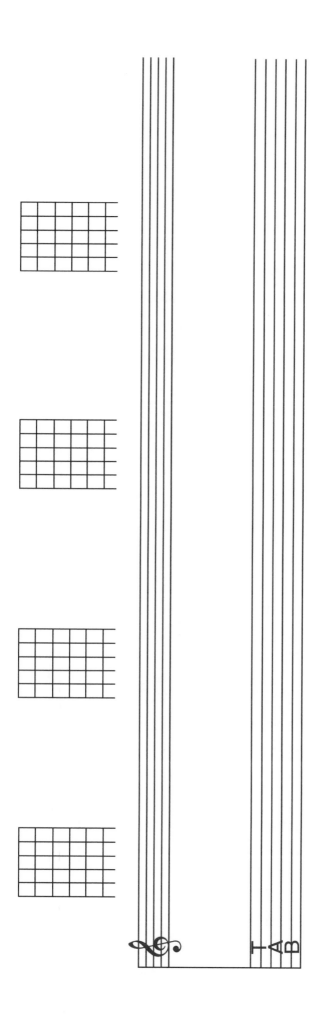

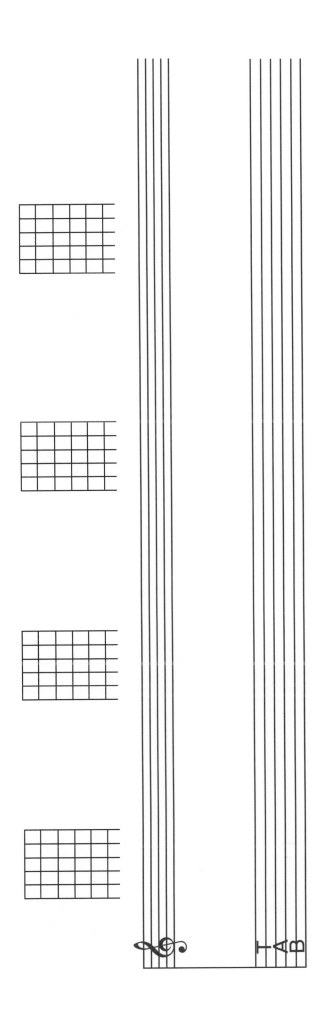

Guitar Tablature Paper

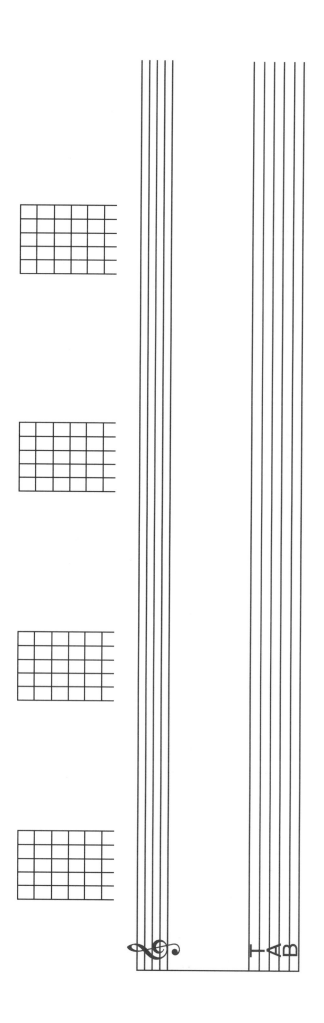

The Guitarist's Handbook

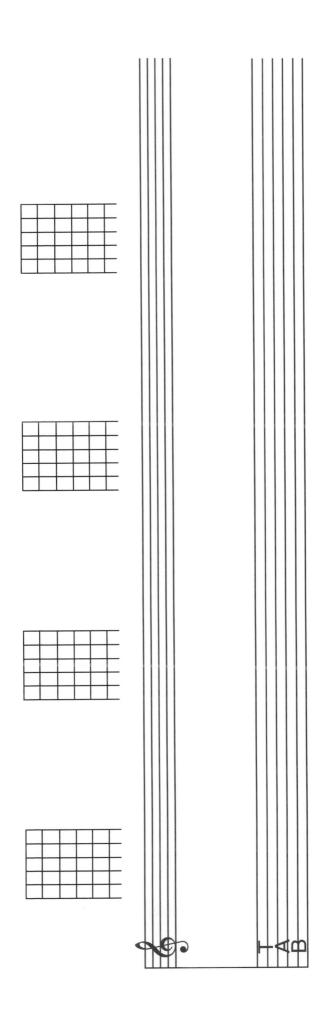

Guitar Tablature Paper

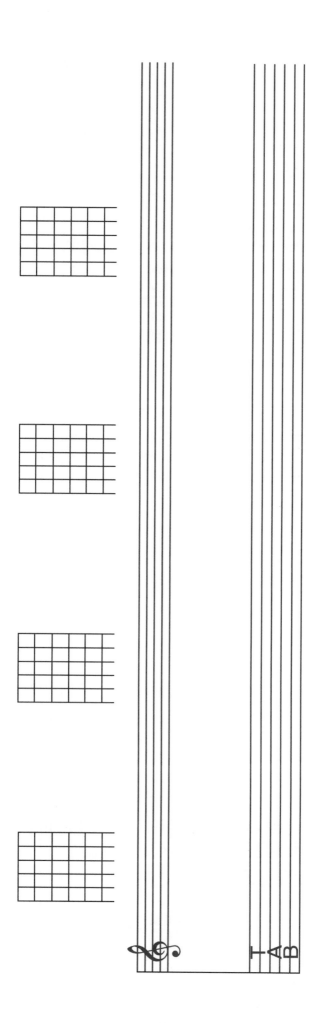

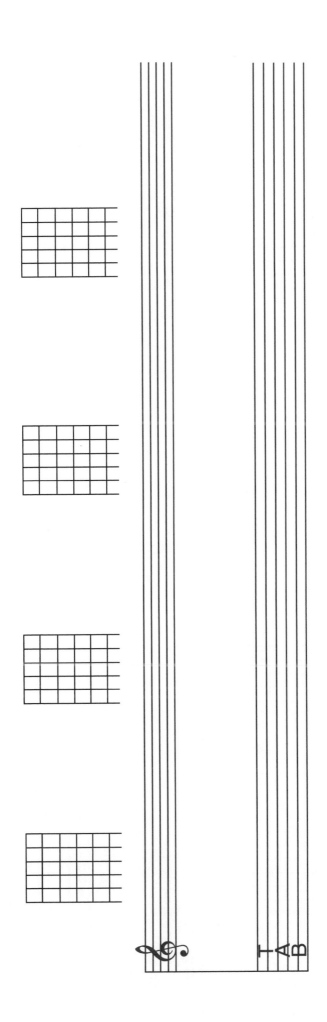

Guitar Tablature Paper

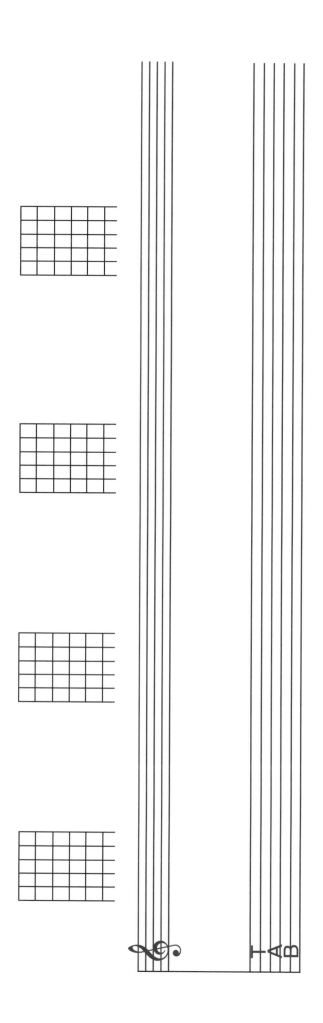

The Guitarist's Handbook

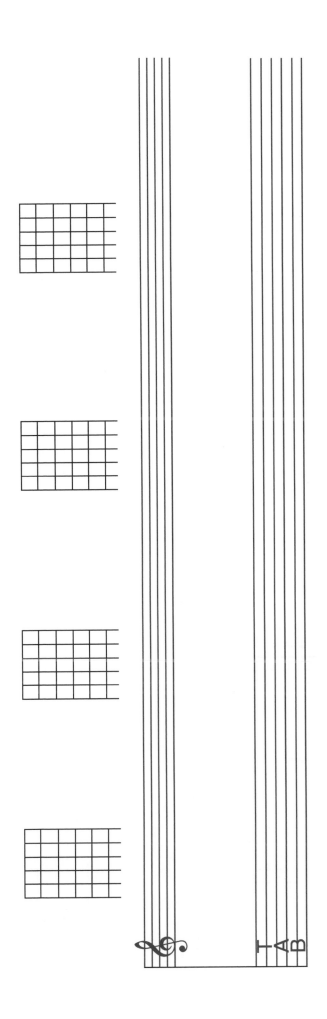

Guitar Tablature Paper

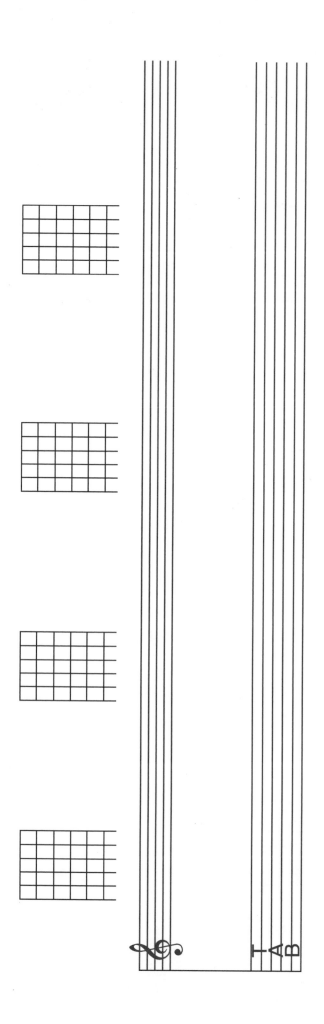

The Guitarist's Handbook